Scientific, Technological and Institutional Aspects of Water Resource Policy

AAAS Selected Symposia Series

 Published by Westview Press, Inc.
5500 Central Avenue, Boulder, Colorado

for the

American Association for the Advancement of Science
1776 Massachusetts Avenue, N.W., Washington, D.C.

Scientific, Technological and Institutional Aspects of Water Resource Policy

Edited by Yacov Y. Haimes

AAAS Selected Symposium **49**

AAAS Selected Symposia Series

This book is based on a symposium which was held at the 1979 AAAS National Annual Meeting in Houston, Texas, January 3-8. The symposium was sponsored by AAAS Sections W (Atmospheric and Hydrospheric Sciences) and X (General) and by two AAAS affiliates, the American Geophysical Union and the American Meteorological Society.

Published in 1980 in the United States of America by
   Westview Press, Inc.
   5500 Central Avenue
   Boulder, Colorado 80301
   Frederick A. Praeger, Publisher

Library of Congress Cataloging in Publication Data
Main entry under title:
Scientific, technological and institutional aspects of water resource policy.
   (AAAS selected symposium ; 49)
   Based on papers presented at a symposium held at the AAAS annual meeting, Houston, Tex., Jan. 3-8, 1979.
   Includes bibliographies and index.
   1. Water resources development--United States--Congresses. I. Haimes, Yacov Y. II. American Association for the Advancement of Science.
III. Series: American Association for the Advancement of Science. AAAS selected symposium ; 49.
HD1694.A5S33   333.91'00973   80-10701
ISBN 0-89158-842-6

Printed and bound in the United States of America

About the Book

This volume addresses water policy issues related to water resources research, ground water, water conservation, urban water systems, water resource planning, supply and demand interaction, principles and standards, and cost-benefit analysis, as well as general, institutional aspects of local, state, regional, and federal policies. The five contributors are scientists with expertise in water resources policy; their associations with Congress, the administration, state and local governments, private industry, and the academic community provide broad perspectives of their subject. The focus of their concerns is the Carter administration's Water Policy Initiatives submitted to Congress in June 1978.

About the Series

The *AAAS Selected Symposia Series* was begun in 1977 to provide a means for more permanently recording and more widely disseminating some of the valuable material which is discussed at the AAAS Annual National Meetings. The volumes in this *Series* are based on symposia held at the Meetings which address topics of current and continuing significance, both within and among the sciences, and in the areas in which science and technology impact on public policy. The *Series* format is designed to provide for rapid dissemination of information, so the papers are not typeset but are reproduced directly from the camera-copy submitted by the authors. The papers are organized and edited by the symposium arrangers who then become the editors of the various volumes. Most papers published in this *Series* are original contributions which have not been previously published, although in some cases additional papers from other sources have been added by an editor to provide a more comprehensive view of a particular topic. Symposia may be reports of new research or reviews of established work, particularly work of an interdisciplinary nature, since the AAAS Annual Meetings typically embrace the full range of the sciences and their societal implications.

WILLIAM D. CAREY
Executive Officer
American Association for
the Advancement of Science

Contents

x   *Contents*

About the Editor and Authors

Yacov Y. Haimes, *professor of systems and civil engineering at Case Western Reserve University, has specialized in modeling and optimization of large-scale systems. He edited* Water Resources and Land Use Planning *(with P. Laconte; The Netherlands: Sijthoff and Noordhoff International Publishers, 1979) and is the author of* Hierarchical Analyses of Water Resources Systems: Modeling and Optimization of Large-scale Systems *(McGraw-Hill, 1977) and* Multiobjective Optimization in Water Resources Systems: The Surrogate Worth Trade-off Method *(with W.A. Hall and H.T. Freedman; Elsevier, 1975). In 1978, as the first American Geophysical Union Congressional Science Fellow, he worked on water policy issues with the Office of Science and Technology Policy and on other water resources and environmental issues with the House Committee on Science and Technology.*

William C. Ackermann *is chief of the Illinois State Water Survey, Institute of Natural Resources, Urbana, Illinois. A registered professional engineer, he has been engaged in water resources research, planning, and data collection and has published widely on these topics. A former director of the American Society of Civil Engineers and a former president of the American Geophysical Union, he has been elected to the National Academy of Engineering and has been awarded the Lincoln Medal.*

Leo M. Eisel *is director of the U.S. Water Resources Council, an independent federal agency which coordinates water resources policy and programs among 31 federal agencies and makes policy recommendations to the President. A former director of the Illinois Environmental Protection Agency and of the Illinois Division of Water Resources, he has had responsibility for development of water resources for flood control, public water usage, navigation, recreation, and fish and wild-life conservation.*

Millard W. Hall, *a civil engineer by training, is chairman of the Missouri River Basin Commission which coordinates the water resources planning activities of nine federal agencies, ten states, and two interstate compact agencies. A former director of the Environmental Studies Center of the University of Maine, he has also served as executive secretary of the Universities Council on Water Resources, an international organization of 90 universities committed to improving water resources research and education. His research activities have focused on plant nutrients in wastewaters, eutrophication in surface waters, industrial wastewater treatment, land and water resources management, and the quantification of airborne pollutants.*

Raymond Kudukis *is president of Kudukis, Schade and Associates, Inc., Cleveland, Ohio. A specialist in civil and environmental engineering, he has participated in numerous conferences and meetings on water policy issues and has received several awards for his work, including the EPA Environmental Quality Award (1974).*

Warren Viessman, Jr., *is a senior specialist in engineering and public works at the Congressional Research Service of the Library of Congress. His specific area of interest is water resources policy. He is a policy analyst and consultant to the U.S. Congress on water policy issues and has published widely in this field.*

The National Water Policy Committee, *American Society of Civil Engineers (ASCE), is composed of* **Frederick J. Clarke,** *Tippetts-Abbett-McCarthy and Stratton (Washington, D.C.);* **Robert D. Henderson,** *Tennessee Valley Authority;* **Victor A. Koelzer,** *Colorado State University;* **Theodore M. Schad,** *National Research Council;* **Verne H. Scott,** *University of California-Davis; and* **Richard W. Karn,** *Bissell & Karn, Inc. (San Leandro, California).*

Preface

The planning and management of our water resources systems are a matter of public policy in that they involve not only scientific and technological considerations, but also economic, political, institutional, legal, and environmental concerns. In recognition of the importance and centrality of these concerns to the scientific community and the public at large, this AAAS volume addresses selected water policy issues from a diversity of perspectives:

- U.S. Congress: Warren Viessman, Jr., Congressional Research Service, Library of Congress;

- National Administration: Leo M. Eisel, U.S. Water Resources Council;

- State Government: William C. Ackermann, Illinois State Water Survey;

- Regional Government: Millard W. Hall, Missouri River Basin Commission;

- Local Government and Private Industry: Raymond Kudukis, formerly with the City of Cleveland Utilities Division and presently with Kudukis and Associates, Cleveland, Ohio;

- Public and Professional Community: The National Water Policy Committee of the American Society of Civil Engineers; and

- Academia: Yacov Y. Haimes, Case Institute of Technology, Case Western Reserve University.

The specific focus of this volume is President Carter's Water Policy Initiatives (WPI) submitted to the Congress

on June 6, 1978. The WPI were developed after intensive
studies and discussions by numerous task forces and public
debates involving federal and state governments and other
sectors of the public. The WPI were issued almost a year
after the President's Environmental Message to Congress,
which called for a review and study of U.S. water resources
policy. Both the study and the WPI generated intense debate
within Congress, the States, and the various public interest
groups. The critical nature and content of these water
resources public policy issues necessarily engender contro-
versy, require broader historical perspectives, and necessi-
tate public examination and debate.

Throughout the years, numerous federal Administrations,
Commissions, and Congresses have addressed the myriad evolving and critical water resource policy issues of respective
times. The conflicts associated with pertinent water resources issues which transcend geographical, sectoral,
societal, environmental, and temporal trade-offs obviate
simple solutions. Cognizant of these complexities, this
volume attempts to analyze, constructively criticize, and
evaluate President Carter's WPI in an historical prospectus;
and to suggest alternative answers to some of the lingering
water resources problems before the nation.

This volume is primarily based on a half-day symposium
entitled "Scientific, Technological, and Institutional Aspects of Water Resource Policy," which was held at the AAAS
Annual Meeting, Houston, Texas, January 3-8, 1979. Although
the summary of Positions on President Carter's WPI --
proposed by the National Water Policy Committee, the American Society of Civil Engineers -- was not included in the
AAAS symposium, the document is included in this volume to
complement the text.

Yacov Y. Haimes
Cleveland, Ohio

Yacov Y. Haimes

1. Research Needs for Water Resources Policy

Abstract

On January 19, 1978, the Office of Science and Technology Policy (OSTP), Executive Office of the President, issued a report which was intended to assist the Policy Committee for Water Resources Policy Study by providing assessment of the scientific and technological aspects of water policy. This paper attempts to evaluate President Carter's Water Policy Initiative of June 6, 1978 in light of the policy recommendations made by OSTP. Two important issues that were not addressed in the President's policy initiatives are discussed here -- ground water and water resources research.

Finally, fifteen future research topics are identified: (1) environmental monitoring; (2) contamination; (3) small communities; (4) standards and regulations; (5) courts; (6) projections; (7) cost effectiveness; (8) value of data; (9) conservation; (10) technology transfer; (11) the other end of research and development; (12) improving universities' institutional set-up; (13) recent environmental laws; (14) ground water; and (15) total systems (holistic) approach.

Preface

"Many presidential messages on domestic policy are somewhat like the final-exam projects of student architects: They are elaborate, finely crafted proposals that show the draftsman's sense of design and his theoretical knowledge of engineering, economics and consumer tastes. They don't show whether his plans will be accepted in the market-place and whether, if carried out, they will stand up. President Carter's message on water policy is of that sort. ...."

From the Washington Post Editorial -- A National Water Policy -- June 8, 1978 [1].

The above statement typified public response to the President's Water Policy Initiatives (WPI) [2]. To fully appreciate the attributes and contributions of the WPI as well as the lack thereof, this paper presents a brief historical background.

Pre-June 6, 1978

In his Environmental Message to the Congress on May 23, 1977, President Carter called for a review and study of water resources policy. He established a Policy Committee for the Water Resources Policy Study [3]. This Committee in turn, set in motion an examination by seven task forces of planning principles and procedures, cost sharing, institutional arrangements, federal reserve rights, research, water quality, and conservation. The analysis by the task forces were to guide the policy determination.

It is worth noting that in 1938, President Roosevelt addressed the Congress on a national plan for the conservation and development of water resources [4]. He recognized then the need for a comprehensive plan and he vetoed a plan that was concerned with, in his words, "limited individual phases of water conservation, with slight regard to other phases." He offered instead a program of water projects on which

"The end to be sought is a unified plan of improvement for each drainage basin in the country, taking into account flood control, pollution abatement, power development, navigation, urban and rural water supply, irrigation, wildlife, recreation and related questions of land management."

Thirty years later, in 1968 Congress established The National Water Commission (in accordance with the provisions of The National Water Commission Act -- Public Law 90-515, approved September 26, 1968). Section 3(a) of P.L. 90-515 identifies the duties of the Commission. Because of its relevance to this discussion, sec. 3(a) is quoted below [5]

"Sec. 3. (a) The Commission shall (1) review present and anticipated national water resource problems, making such projections of water requirements as may be necessary and identifying alternative ways of meeting these requirements--giving consideration, among other things, to conservation and more efficient

use of existing supplies, increased usability by
reduction of pollution, innovations to encourage
the highest economic use of water, interbasin
transfers, and technological advances including,
but not limited to, desalting, weather modification,
and waste water purification and reuse; (2) consider economic and social consequences of water
resource development, including, for example, the
impact of water resource development on regional
economic growth, on institutional arrangement,
and on esthetic values affecting the quality of
life of the American people; and (3) advise on
such specific water resource matters as may be
referred to it by the President and the Water
Resources Council."

The conclusions and recommendations of the National
Water Commission, most of which are just as relevant today
as they were a decade ago, are well-known to all students of
water resources policy [6].

Although limited in its scope on water quality, The National Commission on Water Quality, established pursuant to
Section 315 of The Federal Water Pollution Control Act Amendments of 1972 (Public Law 92-500), contributed in its 1976
report to the shaping of The National Water Policy [7,8].

In 1974, Congress passed the Water Resources Development
Act (Public Law 93-251) [9]. Section 80 (c) of this act
provides that:

"(c) The President shall make a full and complete
investigation and study of principles and standards
for planning and evaluating water and related resources projects. Such investigation and study
shall include, but not be limited to, consideration
of enhancing regional economic development, the
quality of the total environment including its
protection and improvement, the well-being of the
people of the United States, and the national economic development, as objectives to be included in
federally-financed water and related resources projects and in the evaluation of costs and benefits
attributable to such projects, as intended in
section 209 of the Flood Control Act of 1970 (84
Stat. 1818, 1829), the interest rate formula to be
used in evaluating and discounting future benefits
for such projects, and appropriate Federal and non-
Federal cost sharing for such projects. He shall
report the results of such investigation and study,

together with his recommendations, to Congress not
later than one year after funds are first appropriated to carry out this subsection."

The above provision served as one of the stimuli to the
development of the President's WPI.

Finally, as part of the Water Resources Policy Study,
The Office of Science and Technology Policy (OSTP), Executive Office of the President, assisted the President's Policy Committee by providing an assessment of the scientific
and technological aspects of water policy [10]. The two
major goals of the OSTP report are summarized here [11]:

"The OSTP report has two goals. First, the report
attempts to bring into focus the technical and scientific considerations in water policy, including some
technical aspects of organizational management for
problem solving. It is important to bring to bear
on the various issues and options all relevant accum-
ulated scientific knowledge about water resources.
What aspects of hydrology and engineering, for example, set limits on and indicate opportunities for
conservation or improved planning techniques? The
biology of organisms in water that receive pollutants
is vastly better understood than it was just a few
years ago. In what manner can this knowledge be
incorporated in the management of water resources?
The report attempts to summarize the knowledge and
understanding that are available and to make recommendations that derive from them.
    Second, the report attempts to identify the research
directions that address particularly important gaps
in our current knowledge. One of the important results of our changing water problem has been the need
to rework old fields of knowledge. Measures of
efficiency in irrigation water use were designed to
provide guidelines for maximum crop response and give
little guidance for conserving water. We know a lot
about how plants respond to nutrients that are added
to the soil but not much about the fate of the nutrients that the plants did not take up. Plant design
techniques have emphasized minimizing direct 'out of
pocket' costs and now must be reworked to consider
conservation and environmental effects. Technologies
to minimize industrial waste discharges have been
developed at great cost and effort; now they need to
be reevaluated for their cumulative and indirect effects
on the total surface and groundwater system. Where

current knowledge is inadequate to provide guidance
for decisions, further research is required."

Several other studies and reports addressed to national
water policy are listed in the Selected Bibliography section.

June 6, 1978

The President's Water Policy Initiatives of June 6, 1978
were designed to [2]:

1. improve planning and efficient management of federal
    water resource programs to prevent waste and to per-
    mit necessary water projects which are cost-effec-
    tive, safe and environmentally sound to move forward
    expeditiously;

2. provide a new, national emphasis on water con-
    servation;

3. enhance federal-state cooperation and improve state
    water resources planning; and

4. increase attention to environmental quality.

The following is a brief evaluation of the above four
major initiatives. More detailed evaluations of the PWI can
be found elsewhere [12,13].

Planning and Management

The WPI of June 6, 1978 calls for improving the implementation of the Principles and Standards [14] by:

- Requiring the explicit formulation and consideration
  of a primarily non-structural plan as one alternative
  whenever structural water projects or programs are
  planned; and
- Instituting consistent, specific procedures for calculating benefits and costs in compliance with the
  Principles and Standards and other applicable planning
  and evaluation requirements. Benefit-cost analyses
  have not been uniformly applied by Federal agencies,
  and in some cases benefits have been improperly recognized, "double-counted" or included when inconsistent
  with federal policy or sound economic rationale.

The President directed the Water Resources Council to
prepare within 12 months a manual which ensures that benefits and costs are calculated using the best techniques and

provides for consistent application of the Principles and Standards and other requirements. Implicit in the President's recommendations is the recognition of the importance of a multiobjective analysis, where all objectives and attributes of the water system (both commensurable and non-commensurable) should be considered in the analyses.

Water Conservation

The WPI further calls for improving the implementation of the Principles and Standards [14] by adding water conservation as a specific component of both the economic and environmental objectives. The President states [2], "while increases in supply will still be necessary, these reforms place emphasis on water conservation and make clear that this is now a national policy."

Federal-State Cooperation

The WPI declares that the states must be the focal point for water resource management, and that the proposed water reforms are based on this guiding principle. On this initiative, the President states [2], "Therefore I am taking several initiatives to strengthen federal-state relations in the water policy area and to develop a new, creative partnership."

Environmental Quality

The WPI recognizes the importance of environmental quality. The initiatives call for:

a. vigorous implementation of environmental laws,

b. accelerated implementation of Executive Order No. 11988 on flood plain management, which requires the agencies to protect flood plains and to reduce risks of flood losses by not conducting, supporting or allowing actions on flood plains unless there are no practical alternatives,

c. encouraging more effective soil and water conservation through watershed programs of the soil conservation service, and

d. directing the federal agencies to provide increased cooperation with states and leadership in maintaining in-stream flows and protecting ground water through joint assessment of needs, increased assistance in the gathering and sharing of data,

appropriate design and operation of Federal water facilities, and other means.

Post-June 6, 1978

The President's Water Policy Initiatives generated, as
might be expected, a heated debate within Congress, state
governments, and the various sectors of the public (see for
example [1, 12, 13]). Although high expectations were associated with the President's new water policy, many of
which the WPI did not meet. This paper addresses only two
such unfulfilled expectations in two areas:

(1) ground water

(2) water resources research.

Ground Water

In spite of the fact that severe quantity and quality
problems face ground water systems throughout the country,
as ground water resources are contaminated and wells are
closed or depleted, the WPI did not identify specific actions to improve on the planning and management of this
essential water resource.

It is worth noting that ground water is a major source
of water supply in the United States. To dramatize the extent of its importance, a few statistics are useful. For
example, ground water supplies about:

- 24% of all fresh water used in the United States;

- 48% of the total U.S. population;

- 95% of the total domestic, agricultural and industrial needs of the rural population; and

- 50% of all water used for agriculture.

The estimated storage capacity of aquifers (natural under-
ground reservoirs where ground water is held) is nearly 20
times the combined volume of all the nation's rivers, ponds,
and other water on the surface [15,16].

There is also inadequate information about the ground
water resource, leading to increased importance of the
socioeconomic impacts resulting from contamination and
closing of wells. Although considerable progress has been
made in the understanding of water shortage and movement

in aquifer systems, there is inadequate technical data and other information about ground water resources--information which is needed to make sound decisions with regard to regulations and management. Much needs to be done to fully understand the physical and chemical processes involved in the changes of water quality that take place within the aquifer. For instance, changes in quality depend on the original water conditions, on the chemistry of the soils and aquifer formation materials, and on the constituents and pollution loading of incoming waters. Detailed measurements and knowledge of the interactions are essential in all aspects of ground water use and conservation.

Furthermore, the ground water resource is now experiencing a broad and growing focus related to prominent public issues, including among others pollution, energy, water supply, conservation, land use, waste disposal, and urban development. Providing for the protection of the ground water resource, assuring an adequate supply of ground water of good quality, and increasing the efficient use of the ground water resource and its conjunctive management with surface water are essential to national economic stability and growth, and to the well-being of the population. Therefore, the nation's capabilities for technological assessment and planning and policy formulations for ground water resource and its conjunctive use with surface water must be strengthened at both the federal and state levels [16].

Legal and institutional constraints are germane to these ground water problems. In many states, ground water law, like riparian surface water law, is inadequate to allocate the resource among competing users and is unresponsive to the problem of excessive use. The first defect results from the vagueness of the rules of allocation ("unreasonable use") and the second from the failure of the legal system to perceive that ground water is often a common-pool resource in which there is little incentive to save an exhaustible supply for use tomorrow. Any user who seeks to save it is subject to having his saving captured by another pumper from the same aquifer [16].

Recognizing the importance of ground water to the nation's water resources system, and the lack of national water policy pertaining to ground water, the Subcommittee on the Environment and the Atmosphere of the House Committee on Science and Technology developed legislation on ground water Research and Development -- H.R. 13946 [17]. The Bill is

aimed at rectifying past and current dangerous trends toward
fragmented and duplicative efforts by promoting and foster-
ing federal interagency coordination, transfer of technical
information and assistance, training of professionals and
research and development on ground water.

In introducing the above legislation, Congressman George
B. Brown, Jr. stated [16]:

"We fully recognize the intrinsic relationship between
ground and surface water and between water quality and
quantity. The entire water resource program should, of
course, be integrated. As I have cited previously, however, there is good evidence that ground water has been
under-emphasized in the past and it continues to be
under-emphasized now. H.R. 13946, the result of the
Sub-committee's deliberations on the subject, singles
out ground water in recognizing the critical national
value of this vital resource and providing remedies to
past and present inadequacies in ground water research,
development and conjunctive use with surface water.
Because of the severe lag in attention to ground water
problems, an attempt at integration of ground and surface water R. & D. at this late date would be premature
at best. Only after several years of "catch-up" work
could we expect ground water R. & D. to be integrated
with surface water research without harming the ground
water program we envision. We need to work for such
integration and the ground water program should be
carried out with this goal in mind, while maintaining
this long overdue special emphasis for understanding
ground water mandated in the subcommittee's bill, which
I hereby transmit for your attention and information."

Water Resources Research

In spite of the fact that one of the seven task forces
of the Water Resources Policy study was entirely concerned
with water resources research, the President in his WPI did
not address this important issue. Furthermore, one of the
two major goals of the OSTP report, which was aimed at as-
sisting in the formulation of the WPI, was to identify water
research directions [10, 11].

This section attempts to provide a historical background
on water research needs and suggests, as a supplement, fifteen additional research topics.

Historical background. Future need for water resources research has been widely addressed during the last decade. In 1965, President Lyndon B. Johnson asked the Committee on Water Resources Research (COWRR) of the Federal Council for Science and Technology (FCST) to speed the development of a comprehensive, long-range water research program. In February, 1966, FCST published its findings through the Office of Science and Technology, Executive Office of the President. The report, titled "A Ten-Year Program of Federal Water Resources Research," came to be known as 'the Brown Book' [18]. The most interesting and fascinating aspect of the Brown Book is that most of its contents are basically valid today. Of course, the Brown Book does not cover research needs that have become evident since 1966.

In June, 1972, the Universities Council on Water Resources (UCOWR) supported by the Office of Water Resources Research (OWRR) prepared an update of the Brown Book titled "National Water Research Opportunities," [19]. This report was published by the Water Resources Research Institute of the University of Nebraska at Lincoln.

In June, 1973, The National Water Commission identified numerous needs of water resources research [6]. In March, 1976, The National Commission on Water Quality also identified future needs of water resources research [9].

On October 18, 1977, the Office of Science and Technology (OSTP), Executive Office of the President, released in draft form two reports prepared by COWRR that addressed needs of water resources research. These reports are titled "Federal Water Resources Research Program for 1975" [20] and "Directions in U.S. Water Research: 1978-1982" [21].

In January, 1978, in its report to the Policy Committee for the Water Resources Policy Study initiated by President Jimmy Carter, OSTP identified numerous needs for water resources research [10,11]. The OSTP report [10] (and its summary [11]) addressed eleven major topics that include: Climate and Water Supply; Floods and Droughts; Ground Water and its Conjunctive Use with Surface Water; Water Conservation in Irrigation; Water Quality; Erosion and Sedimentation; Water for Energy; New Methods to Increase Water Supply; Future Demands for Water; Urban Water Programs; and A Systems Approach for Water. The major points considered in the OSTP report are summarized below:

•Climate and weather fluctuations are inevitable, and water policy, planning, and management procedures must be devised with this fact in mind.

• Flood protection can best be provided by improved short-term forecasting and associated reservoir management and by increased emphasis on nonstructural measures, such as flood insurance and land use management.

• Drought protection will be enhanced by improved advance planning.

• Ground water is physically related to surface water, and conjunctive management of the two is essential.

• Opportunities exist for substantial conservation of water in agricultural irrigation.

• Greater efforts must be made to control nonpoint sources of pollution, thermal pollution, and salinity.

• Increased efforts are necessary to improve understanding of erosion and sedimentation, and this knowledge should be applied in water planning and management.

• Water may constrain energy production in the future, and energy planners should carefully examine the impact of their plans on other water users.

• No new technologies exist that will substantially increase water supply in the near term.

• Efforts to control demand are an attractive alternative to new investments in water supply.

In April, 1978, the Water Resources Council (WRC) released preliminary volumes of the Second National Water Assessment [22]. In its analysis, the WRC made numerous recommendations on needs of water resources research.

The above national efforts that addressed needs of water resources research on a broad scale have been supplemented over the years by other in-depth studies that have limited scope. Major contributing agencies to this effort include the General Accounting Office, Office of Technology Assessment, House Committee on Science and Technology, Congressional Research Service, Environmental Protection Agency, U.S. Geological Survey, Office of Water Research and Technology, National Science Foundation, National Academy of Sciences, as well as professional societies and many individuals.

With the above historical note, the remainder of this paper attempts to accomplish an almost insurmountable task; namely, to add to and improve upon the presently published needs of water resources research [23].

Future Directions for Water Resources Research

Research should focus on predicting and anticipating the water problems of the 1980's and 1990's, rather than solving the problems of the 1960's and 1970's. Basic research should be made more relevant to solving real, rather than text-book

problems. In particular, the following needs of water
research are identified:

a. Environmental Monitoring

Instead of concentrating on monitoring to control sources
of pollution, R&D efforts should concentrate on discovering
and anticipating environmental problems on a long-term basis.
New environmental problems should be anticipated before they
occur, or at least should be detected in the early stages.
Without such R&D effort, we will continue to be surprised by
environmental crises and will respond hastily with special
studies and hurried legislation, regulations, and enforcement
programs.

b. Contamination

A proper balance should be established between the resources spent to identify pollutants and contaminants, and
the resources spent to remove them. With the development of
the chemical industry (the industry will double its capacity
in 10 years), a new approach is needed to keep the contaminants out of the environment and to reduce the cumulative
impact of toxicants. Furthermore, technology to handle pollutants and contaminants for small communities (e.g. nitrates,
etc.) should be developed.

c. Small Communities

Research should be conducted to find means of alleviating
major financial hardships of small communities that discover
their water (ground or surface) system has been contaminated.
Here, again, a proper balance should be established between
the resources spent on environmental standards and regulations, and the socio-economic impacts of these regulations
on small communities.

d. Standards and Regulations

Extensive R&D should be undertaken to study the scientific and technological basis for standards and regulations and
their socio-economic impacts before they are promulgated.
The level of public acceptance of risk--both voluntary and
involuntary--should be continuously researched.

e. Courts

Most present laws concerning ground water originated in
the judicial branch, not the legislative branch of state
government. By default, judges are determining the laws of

the land in this vital area, and court orders are not necessarily based on sound scientific or technological foundations. Research is needed to (1) Improve the predictability of the legal system. Because of uncertainties about future court actions, effective conjunctive use of ground and surface water cannot be achieved. (2) Determine how judges can best be helped to use available scientific and technological information. (3) Determine how legislators can also be adequately informed about--and induced to base new legislation on--the same essential scientific and technological considerations.

f. Projections

Improved methods are needed to assess, predict, and project water demands and supplies.

g. Cost Effectiveness

Ample methodologies and procedures have been developed for the quantification of costs. Very little has been achieved, however, in developing methodologies for the quantification of benefits--environmental and aesthetic benefits, protection of public health, aversion of risk, etc. Consequently, benefit-cost analysis, which represents only one aspect of the entire evaluation process, still dominates our analyses. Research should be devoted to the quantification of the various noncommensurable objectives and attributes associated with water resources systems. Only then would multiobjective analysis achieve its dominant role in water resource systems analysis [24,25,26].

h. Value of Data

The following questions should be further researched:

How much is a data collection system worth?

How much (data) is enough?

How much monitoring is needed? What elements should be monitored and measured? at what frequency? at what spatial distribution? and for how long?

i. Conservation

The resiliency and robustness of our water resources system are based largely on the BUFFER that the system possesses. Research is needed to study the impacts that conservation might have on the ability of our water resources system to cope with extreme events such as droughts, because of the loss of the existing buffer.

j.   Technology Transfer

Training and continuing education are the key bridges between research and technology transfer. Technology transfer is the mechanism by which research results are transferred to management decisions, planning decisions, and policy decisions. Although several models of technology transfer are available, R&D should be devoted to improvements in: (a) training and retraining of professionals (continuing education); (b) ensuring that there is a receiver at "the other end" for an effective technology transfer; and (c) educating policy- and decision-makers at all levels, including state legislators, judges, administrators, etc.

k.   The Other End of Research and Development

Better procedures should be developed to ensure the proper documentation of research results. Without such procedures, much of our research results are lost, and resources are wasted.

A system of maintenance for mathematical models (similar to the one at the U.S. Army Corps of Engineers, Hydrologic Engineering Center at Davis, California) should be developed. Cars and appliances are marketed with warranties and maintenance services; why should mathematical models be developed without such an essential service.

l.   Improving the Universities' Institutional Set-Up

Interdisciplinary research should be facilitated by removing institutional barriers, e.g.:

- Insure proper credit to junior faculty participating in interdisciplinary R&D (removing the "kiss-of-death" threat).

- Provide incentives to department chairmen to encourage them and their faculty to participate in interdisciplinary R&D.

- Improve regional collaboration among universities.

This subject should be researched, and answers to successful interdisciplinary activities should be developed.

m.   Recent Environmental Laws

Research should be conducted to assess the socio-economic impacts of recent environmental laws such as the "National

Environmental Policy Act of 1969 (P.L. 91-180), the "Federal
Water Pollution Control Act Amendments of 1972" (P.L. 92-500),
the Endangered Species Act of 1973" (P.L. 93-205), the Safe
Drinking Water Act" (P.L. 93-527) [28], the "Resource Conservation and Recovery Act of 1976" (P.L. 94-580) [27], the
"Clean Water Act of 1977" (P.L. 95-217) [29], and others.
There is also a need for R&D to identify the contradictions
among these laws, establish their scientific and technological basis, and evaluate the need to amend them to meet the
problems of the 1980's and 1990's.

n. Ground Water

Current expenditures on Federal Water Resource Research
is about $230 million per year. Of this, only $12-13 million
is being spent on ground-water R&D.

The recent Bill (H.R. 13946), which was introduced in the
House of Representatives in August 1978, articulated major
ground-water R&D needs [17]. Extensive R&D efforts are
required to investigate quality and contamination problems,
as well as quantity problems.

o. Total Systems (Holistic) Approach

Our response to the ever-increasing complexity and scale
of water and related problems should be the adoption of the
total systems (Holistic) approach. We should stop separating

• Water quantity from water quality

• Surface water from ground water

• Water resources from land resources

• Scientific and technological considerations from
   institutional, legal, economic and environmental
   considerations.

Responsive R&D in this area is needed.

In summary, although many of the fifteen research topics
discussed in this paper have been intensively investigated
and studied for a long time, recent societal and technological changes have brought new dimensions to old problems.
Consequently, both basic and applied research are needed to
provide long- and short-term answers to the above water and
related land resources issues.

Concluding Comments

A sound national water resource policy should recognize the intrinsic relationship between water as a resource, and all other elements that relate to human activities, and to nature. Furthermore, a sound national water resource policy can be developed only if the interrelationships among the components of the water resources system and issues are understood; if the needs for research and development are articulated; if the goals and objectives of the various con- stituents are recognized; if the needs and future plans of the various sectors of the economy are accounted for; if the current federal, regional, state and local organizational structure is understood; if the real constraints and impacts of existing water laws are appreciated; and finally, if the role that hydrologic, climatic, engineering and other scientific disciplines can and should play in the development of water resource policy is properly investigated and facilitated. Such a sound water resource policy should add both robustness and resiliency to our water resources systems, so that inevitable periods of droughts or floods may have the least adverse effect on man, the environment, and the economy.

References

[1] The Washington Post, "A National Water Policy — Editorial," Washington, D.C., June 8, 1978.

[2] The President of the United States, "Federal Water Policy Initiatives," U.S. Government Printing Office, June 6, 1978.

[3] Carter, J., Environmental Message to Congress, The White House, Washington, D.C., May 23, 1977.

[4] Brown, George E., Jr., "Luncheon Address at the Symposium on National Water Policy," Proceedings and Workshop Reports, Symposium on National Water Policy, sponsored by the Metrek Division of the MITRE Corporation, Washington, D.C., May 15-17, 1978, pp. 27-31.

[5] The National Water Commission Act, Public Law 90-515, September 26, 1968. Also see Appendix I of the Final Report to the President by the Commission [6].

[6]   National Water Commission, Water policies for the
      future, Final Report to the President and to the
      Congress of the United States, U.S. Government Printing
      Office, Washington, D.C., June 1973.

[7]   The Federal Water Pollution Control Act Amendments of
      1972, Public Law 92-500, October 18, 1972.

[8]   National Commission on Water Quality, Report to the
      Congress by the National Commission on Water Quality,
      Stock Number 052-003-0153-5, U.S. Government Printing
      Office, Washington, D.C., March 18, 1976.

[9]   The Water Resources Development Act of 1974, Public Law
      93-251, March 7, 1974.

[10] Office of Science and Technology Policy, "Scientific
      and Technological Aspects of Water Resource Policy,"
      Executive Office of the President, Washington, D.C.,
      January 19, 1978.

[11] Ackermann, William C.; Allee, David J.; Amorocho,
      Jaime; Haimes, Yacov Y.; Hall, Warren A.; Messerve,
      Richard A.; Patrick, Ruth; and Smith, Philip M.,
      "Scientific and Technological Considerations in Water
      Resources Policy," EOS Transactions of the American
      Geophysical Union, Vol. 59, No. 6, June 1978.

[12] Committee on Energy and Natural Resources, U.S. Senate,
      "The Water Resources Policy Study: An Assessment,"
      Publication No. 95-108, June 1978.

[13] Viessman, Warren, Jr., "An Analysis of the President's
      Water Policy Initiatives," Congressional Research
      Service, Library of Congress, 78-138 ENR, June 26, 1978.

[14] Water Resources Council, "Water and Related Land
      Resources: Establishment of Principles and Standards
      for Planning," Federal Register, September 10, 1973.

[15] Haimes, Y. Y. and Spensley, J. W., "Ground-Water
      Quality--A Public Health Hazard?" Invited Paper present-
      ed at the Spring Meeting of the American Physical
      Society, Washington, D.C., April 24-27, 1978.

[16] Committee on Science and Technology, U.S. House of
      Representatives, "Ground-Water Quality Research and
      Development," Hearings (Including Report) before the
      Subcommittee on the Environment and the Atmosphere,
      Report No. 80, 1978.

[17]   U.S. House of Representatives, H.R. 13946, A Bill Introduced by Congressman George E. Brown, Jr. of California, August 17, 1978.

[18]   Committee on Water Resources Research, Federal Council for Science and Technology, Office of Science and Technology, "A Ten-Year Program of Federal Water Resources Research ('Brown Book'), Executive Office of the President, Washington, D.C., February 1966.

[19]   Water Resources Research Institute, National water research opportunities, A Report to the Office of Water Resources Research, U.S. Department of the Interior, Univ. of Nebraska, Lincoln, June 1972.

[20]   Committee on Water Resources Research, Federal Coordinating Council for Science, Engineering, and Technology, Office of Science and Technology Policy, "Federal Water Resources Research Program for 1975" (draft), Executive Office of the President, Washington, D.C., October 1977.

[21]   Committee on Water Resources Research, Federal Coordinating Council for Science, Engineering, and Technology, Office of Science and Technology Policy, Directions in U.S. water research: 1978-1982, Main report and summary report (draft), Executive Office of the President, Washington, D.C., October 1977.

[22]   Water Resources Council, "The Nation's Water Resources: The Second National Water Assessment," (review copy), Washington, D.C., April 1978.

[23]   Haimes, Y. Y., "Future Needs of Water Resources Research," Invited paper presented at the Annual Meeting of Universities Council on Water Resources (UCOWR), Urbana, Illinois, August 1, 1978.

[24]   Haimes, Y. Y., Hall, W. A., and Freedman, F. T., Multiobjective Optimization in Water Resource Systems: The Surrogate Worth Trade-Off Method, Elsevier Scientific Publishing Co., 1975.

[25]   Cohon, J. L., Multiobjective Programming and Planning, Academic Press, N.Y., 1978.

[26]   Haimes, Y. Y., Hierarchical Analyses of Water Resources Systems: Modeling and Optimization of Large-Scale Systems, McGraw-Hill International Book Company, 1977.

[27] Resource Conservation and Recovery Act of 1976, Public
      Law 94-580, October 21, 1976.

[28] Safe Drinking Water Act, Public Law 93-523, December
      16, 1974.

[29] Clean Water Act of 1977, Public Law 95-217, December
      27, 1977.

Selected Bibliography

1. Committee on Erosion and Sedimentation, AGU Hydrology
    Section, Research Needs in Erosion and Sedimentation,
    EOS Trans. AGU, 58(12), 1076-1083, 1977.

2. Federal Register, "Water Resources Council, Water
    Resource Policy Study Issue and Option Papers," July 15,
    1977 and July 25, 1977.

3. General Accounting Office, Groundwater: An overview,
    Rep. CED-77-69, Washington, D.C., June 21, 1977.

4. General Accounting Office, More and better uses could
    be made of billions of gallons of water by improving
    irrigation delivery systems, Rep. CED-77-117, Washington,
    D.C., September 2, 1977.

5. Holcomb Research Institute, Butler University, Utiliza-
    tion of numerical ground-water models for water resources
    management, Report Prepared for the Scientific Committee
    on Problems of the Environment (SCOPE) and the U.S.
    Environmental Protection Agency, Indianapolis, Ind.,
    December 5, 1977.

6. Office of Water Research and Technology, Final report on
    research goals and objectives, U.S. Department of the
    Interior, Washington, D.C., December 15, 1976.

7. Office of Water Research and Technology and the Water
    Resources Research Institutes, "Water Resource Problems
    and Research Needs, FY 1978, Summary of State and
    Regional Water Resources Research Needs, Washington, D.C.
    October 1, 1976.

8. Panel on Water and Climate, Geophysics Study Committee,
    Geophysics Research Board, Assembly of Mathematical and
    Physical Sciences, National Research Council, "Climate,
    Climatic Change, and Water Supply, Study in Geophys.,"
    National Academy of Sciences, Washington, D.C., 1977.

9. Special Projects Division, Soil Conservation Service, "Crop Consumptive Irrigation Requirements and Irrigation Efficiency Coefficients for the United States," U.S. Department of Agriculture, Washington, D.C., June 1976.

10. U.S. Committee for the Global Atmospheric Research Program, National Research Council, "Understanding Climatic Change, A Program for Action," National Academy of Sciences, Washington, D.C., 1975.

11. U.S. Water Resources Council, "Water for Energy Self-Sufficiency," Washington, D.C., October 1974.

12. U.S. Water Resources Council, "Summary of Public Comments on Hearings Related to the Water Resource Policy Study," from July 19, 1977 to September 23, 1977, unpublished, 1977.

13. Universities Council on Water Resources and the Engineering Foundation, "Workshop Report: Integrating Water Quality and Water and Land Resources Planning," Cornell University, Ithaca, N.Y., August, 1976.

14. Water Resources Research Institute, "Reorientation of Urban Water Resources Research," Rutgers, The State University of New Jersey, New Brunswick, February, 1976.

2. An Overview of National Water Policy

Abstract

The President's water policy, introduced June 6, 1978, suggests a drive by the Executive Branch to gain greater control over Federal spending for large dams and other water projects. It calls for tougher standards in the evaluation of Federal water projects and increased cost sharing by non-federal participants. Strengthening of environmental considerations in water resources development and establishment of conservation as a principal component of the primary objectives of water resources planning are also included. The policy statement was silent, however, on the issue of the massive Federal water pollution control program and its relationship to other aspects of water resources management and development.

Background

President Carter's 1977 environmental message to Congress started an intensive review of national water policy. The Administration published "issues and options" in the Federal Register (July 1977) and held eight regional hearings. These generated much comment, especially from water interests in the western states. In response, the Senate passed a resolution expressing its concern about interference with the traditional state role in water allocation actions.

Then, on June 6, 1978, President Carter presented his Water Policy Initiatives (WPI) to the Congress. He stated that his policy was designed to:

- improve planning and management of federal water resources programs,

- Emphasize water conservation,

- Enhance federal-state cooperation, and

- Increase attention to environmental quality. (1)

This paper reviews the progress made in implementing the new water policy and summarizes the major water resources issues before the 96th Congress.

Highlights of the President's Water Policy

Planning and Evaluation

In considering the adequacy of the water resources planning objectives, the President proposed that national economic development and environmental quality be retained and weighted equally. He also added conservation to these objectives.

Economic analysis of water projects was emphasized, and it was stated that implementation of the Principles and Standards (P & S) would be improved by instituting consistent procedures for calculating benefits and costs. The lack of P & S coverage of federally-assisted projects was not addressed, however, and this is surprising, considering that federal grants and loans for water projects now exceed direct federal funding.

The WPI sidestepped the politically volatile and often-debated issue of the discount rate, but it did come to grips with the problem of non-uniformity in project planning and evaluation procedures. The President also announced that an independent review function would be assigned to the Water Resources Council.

Cost Sharing

Cost sharing is a key element of national water policy. The President aims to achieve greater state involvement in water project decisions and eliminate conflicting cost sharing rules. His proposals suggest greater consistency than now exists, but in most cases, variations in cost sharing levels among purposes, programs and agencies are not eliminated; instead an additional 5 to 10 percent charge upon existing arrangements is superimposed.

Institutions

The need to avoid impairment of environmental values was another area stressed. Protection of instream flows for

recreation, water quality, aesthetics, and fish and wildlife
habitats was emphasized. Needed improvements in water management associated with the relationship between groundwater and
surface water and the relationship between water quantity and
water quality were also recognized but no substantive actions
were proposed.

Conservation

Methods for combating inefficient water use were given
high priority. The President set forth several initiatives
to encourage conservation including pricing, technical assistance and federal program reforms. He also called for improvement of irrigation repayment and water service contract
procedures under existing authorities of the Bureau of Reclamation (BR).

There is merit in the WPI's suggested imposition of conservation measures as a condition for grant and loan programs, but determining the nature of these and how to impose
them is quite another matter. The President's water policy
is not clear on this. Well-intentioned as his proposals
seem, severe adverse effects could result if economic, tech-
nologic, social and institutional impacts are not thoroughly
considered.

Water Quality

Considering the importance of water quality to the
nation and the portion of the federal water budget devoted
to this area (over 50 percent), it is surprising that the WPI
had little to say on this matter. The fact that water
quantity-water quality issues must be dealt with jointly
will have to take hold if efficient water management and
development are to occur. It seems that the goals of water
quality management should be considered in the context of a
comprehensive policy for total water management. (2)

Federal Reserved and Indian Water Rights

Finally, the President has instructed federal agencies
to work promptly and expeditiously to inventory and quantify
federal reserved and Indian water rights. This problem has
its greatest dimension in western areas where some states
have been unable to allocate water because these rights are
not defined. Negotiation rather than litigation is to be
emphasized.

Implementation of the Water Policy

To implement his water policy, President Carter issued 13 Directives on July 12, 1978. These covered the following subjects:

- Improved planning and evaluation of federal water resources programs and projects,

- Environmental quality and water resources management,

- Non-structural flood protection methods,

- Enhanced federal-state cooperation in water management,

- Federal and Indian reserved water rights,

- Water conservation and floodplain management in federal programs,

- Conservation pricing of water supplied by federal projects,

- Technical assistance for water conservation in water-short areas,

- Water conservation in housing assistance programs,

- Water conservation at federal facilities,

- Water conservation provisions in loan and grant programs for water supply and treatment,

- Agricultural assistance programs in water-short areas, and

- Improvements in soil conservation service programs.

The implementation phase involves several strategies. Some elements of the WPI require new legislation; others require new regulations under existing authority; while the remainder can be accomplished through various administrative changes.

Nineteen federal interagency task forces were formed to carry out the 13 initiatives. Each is headed by a lead agency and is composed of representatives from other involved agencies. The Secretary of the Interior has been given the responsibility to see that the initiatives are carried out expeditiously.

The status of completion of task force assignments can be subdivided into three categories:

- The first of these is one in which preliminary reports or option papers are completed but possible regulations, guidelines or other studies are to follow. Topics in this group include nonstructural flood control, technical assistance for water conservation in water-short areas, water conservation in housing assistance programs, water conservation at federal facilities, water conservation in loan and grant programs for water treatment and waste water, agricultural assistance in water-short areas, and improvements in Soil Conservation Service (SCS) programs. The task forces having these assignments are circulating their preliminary reports for public comment, holding regional meetings and consulting with the Congress and the states. The reports and recommended actions will be reviewed by the Secretary of the Interior, the Water Resources Council (WRC), Office of Management and Budget (OMB), or Council on Environmental Quality (CEQ) as called for in the Presidential Directives. Initial reviews were scheduled to be completed by April 1, 1979 with further reviews to follow as proposed actions are published in the Federal Register.

- The second category is one in which draft legislation is being readied for consideration by Congress. Bills on technical and planning assistance to states, cost sharing improvements and state conservation pricing options are being prepared by the Administration. It is expected that the proposed legislation will be introduced early in 1979.

- The last category is that in which studies have longer lead times and most final products are not expected until mid or late 1979. The following subjects fall into this classification: changes in the P & S, Fish and Wildlife Coordination Act regulations, National Historic Preservation Act regulations, environmental statutes compliance report, groundwater and instream flows, federal reserved water rights, Indian reserved water rights, water conservation - Phase II, floodplain management and conservation pricing.

A final aspect of implementation is embodied in Executive

Order 12113, dated January 4, 1979. This order directed WRC
to ensure that an impartial technical review is performed on
pre-authorization reports or proposals and preconstruction
plans for federal and federally-assisted water and related
land resources projects and programs. Beginning April 1,
1979, it will be mandatory for agencies to submit plans and
reports on projects to WRC for review.

Those aspects of implementing the WPI which require new
legislation will bear close scrutiny as bills are introduced
in Congress and hearings proceed. In particular, the cost
sharing proposals are likely to be quite controversial. Other
aspects of implementation which may have far-reaching implications are those regulations and legislative initiatives
which will focus on conservation practices and environmental
considerations such as instream flow maintenance.

Water Policy Issues Before the 96th Congress

The 96th Congress will be facing a return of many old
water resources issues and several new ones resulting from
the President's water policy.

Issues Expected to Be Addressed Early in the 96th Congress

Reorganization of Natural Resources Programs. The
history of natural resource reorganization dates back to the
"Ash Council" proposals of 1971 (92nd Congress) which urged
the consolidation of seven major departments into four. One
proposal was to establish a Department of Natural Resources.
Although hearings were held, no Congressional action was
taken. In the 93rd Congress, the concept of a natural resources department re-emerged but the focus soon turned ex-
clusively to energy. The outgrowth was the Department of
Energy (DOE).

In 1977, President Carter directed OMB to undertake a
major review of natural resources reorganization options.
This was completed, and a proposal from the President was
announced on March 1, 1979.

Although several reorganization plans were considered,
the popular and sweeping option for reorganization would have
included all agencies and functions of the Interior Department, except for the Bureau of Reclamation's water project
construction which would have gone to the Army Corps of Engineers. The Corps would have lost its role in planning and
authorizing civilian civil works projects but would have
functioned as the building arm of the new Cabinet department.

The Agriculture Department's Forest Service and SCS would also have been transferred to the new department, along with the Commerce Department's National Oceanic and Atmospheric Administration (NOAA). The WRC and the independent Marine Mammal Commission would have been other additions to the Department of Natural Resources (DNR).

As a result of intense political pressure, the President revised his reorganization plan to exclude elements of the major water construction and planning agencies from the DNR. The newly-proposed department will now consist of all functions of the old Department of Interior plus the U.S. Forest Service and NOAA.

The establishment of the Natural Resources Department will be sought under the President's reorganization authority, giving Congress 60 days to block the plan. If neither House acts, the plan goes into effect automatically.

Conservation. Changes in institutions such as property rights, organizations and social customs appear needed to effect systematic, large-scale conservation, but incremental changes could be made for new water developments with minimal disruption of current policies and practices. For example, loans by the Farmers Home Administration to finance private irrigation development could carry a restriction requiring that new facilities be designed and operated using the best available conservation practices. (3)

Various conservation tactics can be employed. These include:

- Incentives in the form of subsidies, tax relief and increased earnings for implementation of proven conservation practices,

- Economic measures such as pricing policies, taxation and fines,

- Regulation of new developments,

- Structural modification of existing facilities, and

- Modification of current operating practices.

Based on the WPI, numerous proposals related to conservation are expected to emerge. Some of these will likely result in new legislation while others may be accommodated by rules and regulations under existing authorities. The impact of these proposals will bear monitoring.

Cost Sharing. Although the need for cost sharing reform has long been recognized, developers and beneficiaries of water programs have strongly resisted change. (4)

The cost sharing issue is fundamentally one of determining the proportion of costs for water resources control, management and development which various beneficiaries should bear. A draft bill designed along the lines of the President's June 6 message has been prepared by WRC, but to date, has not been introduced in the Congress.

Waterway User Charges. A reoccurring question is: should the schedule of inland waterway user charges established during the 95th Congress be increased or decreased?

The Inland Waterways Revenue Act of 1978 for the first time levies a waterway user charge or a fuel tax on commercial freight traffic traveling on inland waterways. The legislation also requires an extensive study of future policy alternatives for the Upper Mississippi River and a study of the economic impact of waterway user charges on several transportation sectors. A bill to increase the already-imposed user fees has been introduced in the 96th Congress (H.R. 1481). The enactment of P.L. 95-502 seems to have signaled the start of a new movement by the Congress to reevaluate this nation's water resources policies.

Authorization and Appropriations for Water Resources Projects. The President's budget for fiscal 1980 continues his effort to limit the water project pork barrel. The Administration believes that most worthwhile water resource projects are already built or underway. Only 26 new construction starts for the coming year have been recommended.

The total cost of completing these projects is $578 million, a small amount when compared with the backlog of projects currently underway, which the Administration estimates will cost $42.5 billion by the time they are completed.

In his 1980 budget proposal, the President includes $2.6 billion in budget authority to advance the work on the backlog of projects and to provide the full cost of completing the 26 new projects he has recommended.

It is expected that many members of Congress will again resist the President's excursion into water project selection. The battle begun in the 95th Congress over water project starts will continue.

Clean Water Act (P.L. 95-217). Congress is expected to

hold oversight hearings on the Clean Water Act during both sessions. It is likely that this $4-5 billion a year program will become the target of inflation fighters. States will probably seek full funding, but there may be conflicting demands on how the money is to be spent. Drinking water treatment construction programs are an option being considered.

Safe Drinking Water Act (P.L. 93-523). The issue here is that the mandates of the Safe Drinking Water Act are expected to clash with concerns about costs of government regulations and the Administration's push for fiscal austerity.

Other issues expected to receive early attention by the 96th Congress are:

- Increasing from $3 million to $25 million the annual funding of state water planning under the existing 50-50 percent matching program administered by the WRC (P.L. 89-90),

- Legislation to provide $25 million annually in 50-50 percent matching grant assistance to states to implement water conservation technical assistance programs,

- Acreage limitation on agricultural lands under contract with the Bureau of Reclamation,

- Federal reserved and Indian water rights,

- Groundwater management,

- Rural water supply and wastewater disposal systems,

- Pacific Northwest Power marketing, and

- Coordination of planning processes and implementation of river basin and regional plans.

Issues Expected to Be Addressed by the Congress in the Near Future

Looking ahead, additional issues expected to be addressed by the Congress include:

- Agricultural non-point source pollution,

- Application of Principles and Standards to federally-assisted projects,

- Coordination of water quantity-water quality planning,

- Future role of the Bureau of Reclamation,

- Instream flow determinations,

- Water resources subsidies,

- Roles of federal, state and local governments in water resources planning, development and management, and

- Revitalization of urban water supply systems.

A final issue is the reassessment of water quality management goals. Here, consideration may ultimately be given to a shift from the present technological-fix orientation to one which focuses on setting regional water quality goals and practical procedures for achieving them.

Summary

The President's water policy, introduced June 6, 1978, suggests a drive by the Executive Branch to gain greater control over federal spending for large dams and other water projects. It calls for tougher standards in the evaluation of federal water projects and increased cost sharing by non-federal participants. Strengthening of environmental considerations in water resources development and establishment of conservation as a principal component of the primary objectives of water resources planning are also included. The policy statement was silent, however, on the issue of the massive federal water pollution control program and its relationship to other aspects of water resources management and development.

To implement his water policy, President Carter issued 13 Directives on July 12, 1978. These involve several strategies: new legislation, new regulations under existing authority, and administrative changes. Bills on technical and planning assistance to states, cost sharing improvements, and state conservation pricing options are being prepared by the Administration for introduction in the 96th Congress early in 1979. Furthermore, effective April 1, 1979, the Water Resources Council was directed to conduct an impartial technical review of pre-authorization reports or proposals and preconstruction plans for federal and federally-assisted water and related land resources projects and programs.

Of the issues expected to be given early consideration by the Administration and the 96th Congress, many have significant technical overtones. These include conservation, groundwater management, drinking water standards, water project selection, instream flow evaluation, allocation of water supplies, water quality management, cost sharing, water resources planning, and non-point source pollution. In most cases, there is still time for the public to influence future regulations or legislation.

Finally, the extent to which the President's water policy is implemented will depend, in large measure, on the willingness of Congress to cooperate.

References

1. Carter, Jimmy, Federal Water Policy Initiatives, House Document No. 95-347, U.S. Govt. Print. Off., Washington, D.C., June 6, 1978, 8 pp.
2. Universities Council on Water Resources (UCOWR), Workshop Report: Integrating Water Quality and Water and Land Resources Planning, Cornell University, Ithaca, New York, August 1976, 338 pp.
3. Universities Council on Water Resources (UCOWR), Review of Water Resources Policy Options, University of Nebraska, Lincoln, Nebraska, October 1977, 38 pp.
4. National Water Commission (NWC), Water Policies for the Future, Washington, D.C., U.S. Govt. Print. Off., 1973, 579 pp.

3. Improving Procedures for Planning and Evaluating Federal Water Resources Projects

Abstract

In July 1978, the President gave several directives to the U.S. Water Resources Council including: (1) revise the "Principles and Standards for Planning Water and Related Land Resources" and produce a procedures manual for agency implementation of the Principles and Standards, and (2) implement an independent review of water resource projects proposed for construction by Federal agencies. The objective of both these directives is to improve the water resources planning of Federal agencies thereby insuring that economically efficient and environmentally sound projects will be given priority for construction. Economic analysis limitations and institutional constraints have the potential for reducing the effectiveness of these reform efforts. Technology and institutional limitations can also affect the implementation of other Presidential directives to the Water Resources Council such as the implementation of a water conservation technical assistance program for the States.

Introduction

Over the past two years, there has been considerable Federal activity in management of the Nation's water resources. A focal point of this activity has been the initiation and implementation of a review of Federal water policy by the Carter Administration.

Much of the effort in the water policy review has concentrated on improving the procedures for planning and evaluation of Federal water resources programs and projects. In July 1978, the President directed the Water Resources Council to carry out certain actions designed to improve the planning and evaluation procedures used by Federal water resources

agencies. Implementation of this Presidential directive has
focused on improving and updating procedures used for benefit-cost analysis. Planning and evaluation of Federal water
resources programs and projects have long depended on benefit-cost analysis as a means to quantify expected benefits
and costs resulting from proposed projects or programs.

Much of the early benefit-cost development work in the
United States was done in association with proposed water
resources projects and benefit-cost analysis is probably
further advanced in water resources than in other comparable
areas. While there have been recent developments in benefit-
cost analysis, for example with regard to estimating recreation benefits, the majority of the theory and procedures for
benefit-cost analysis was developed in the 1960's or earlier.
However, the problem still remains of how to transfer this
theory into practice given the constraints of time, data and
computation ability.

Deficiencies of the Principles and Standards

While much has been done to advance the use of benefit-
cost analysis in water resources, various shortcomings still
exist. At the present time, the various Federal water resources construction agencies plan and evaluate projects
according to the general guidelines of the Principles and
Standards for Planning of Water and Related Land Projects,
which were published by the United States Water Resources
Council in 1973. The Principles and Standards are, as their
name implies, a set of general procedures for planning water
resources projects and doing benefit-cost analyses. Each
of the Federal construction agencies; the U.S. Army Corps of
Engineers, the Bureau of Reclamation, the Soil Conservation
Service, and the Tennessee Valley Authority; has developed
its own set of detailed rules, regulations and procedures
for performing benefit-cost analysis and water resources
planning in compliance with the Principles and Standards.
This has led to a situation in which the procedures used by
each agency for water resources planning and benefit-cost
analysis are not consistent and employ a generally wide
range of methods.

Another deficiency with the Principles and Standards is
that they do not cover a major portion of Federal water resources management and development programs. At present,
the Principles and Standards do not cover the loan and grant
programs of the EPA, Farmers Home Administration, Economic
Development and Assistance Program of the Department of
Commerce, Community Development Block Grants Program, Rural
Electrification Administration, and other Federal assistance

programs which have a substantial impact on the management,
development and conservation of the Nation's water resources.
The Principles and Standards presently only cover those
projects directly implemented by the Federal Government such
as the various water resource development projects of the
Corps, Bureau of Reclamation, Soil Conservation Service and
TVA. This is not to say that coverage of the Principles and
Standards in their present form should be immediately extended to the EPA treatment facilities grants program or that
the existing Principles and Standards are appropriate for application to the federally-assisted programs. Rather, the
point is that only about 30 percent of the annual Federal
water resources development budget is presently covered by
the Principles and Standards.

Acknowledged technical deficiencies exist in the procedures used for benefit-cost analysis. Similarly, the data
requirements for many of the existing procedures are such
that necessary data cannot be obtained by field level people
operating under their individual budget and staff constraints.
Furthermore, the existing Principles and Standards are primarily intended for analysis and evaluation of traditional
structural projects, such as reservoirs and pumping stations,
with little emphasis on the so-called "nonstructural" type
of project, involving floodplain management and water conservation measures.

Another deficiency with the benefit-cost analysis presently performed by Federal water resource construction agencies in accordance with the Principles and Standards is the
sometimes lack of credibility by the general public in the
benefit-cost analysis. One of the causative factors responsible for this problem is that the public perceives that the
benefit-cost analysis is now performed by the same construction agency that will benefit from additional proposed
projects. No other entity, except the Office of Management
and Budget, reviews the benefit-cost analysis performed by
the Federal construction agency, and the review by OMB is
often suspect because of the acknowledged bias of OMB toward
reducing Federal expenditures for water resources projects.

Implementation of the Presidential Directives

The water problems of the 1970's, and presumably those
of the 1980's, will continue to place new demands on planning and evaluation procedures. If benefit-cost analysis is
to play a meaningful role in water resources management decisions in the 1980's, it must be capable of analyzing solutions which integrate ground and surface water management
as well as water quality and quantity. Benefit-cost proce-

dures must be unbiased with respect to nonstructural measures. We no longer have the luxury of simply evaluating the
benefits and costs associated with a single reservoir. However, in the end, the question is the same. Which programs
and projects should be funded? What level of funding is appropriate? What projects and programs should be built now
and which should be deferred until later?

In order to meet these various problems and deficiencies, the President directed the Water Resources Council in
July 1978 to revise certain aspects of the Principles and
Standards in order to place more emphasis on nonstructural
solutions to water resources problems and to insure more
adequate consideration of water conservation. Specifically,
the President directed:

"In order to provide greater consideration of
water conservation and non-structural alternatives
in all projects and programs subject to the Principles and Standards, the Water Resources Council
is directed to modify the Principles and Standards
in the following respects:

• The Principles and Standards shall be modified
to accomplish the full integration of water
conservation into project and program planning
and review, as a component of both the economic
development and environmental quality objectives,
and

• The Principles and Standards shall be modified
to require the preparation and inclusion of a
primarily non-structural plan as one alternative
whenever structural project or program alternatives are considered. This alternate plan should
incorporate a combination of non-structural or
demand reducing measures which could feasibly
be employed or adopted to achieve the overall
project purpose. Such measures should not be
limited to those which the agency of the Federal
government could implement directly under present
authority but should including floodplain management techniques (such as zoning), pricing policies,
groundwater recharge, and other measures."

The President further directed the Water Resources Council
to complete a manual of procedures for water resources planning and benefit-cost analysis which would be used by all
Federal water resources development agencies:

"The Water Resources Council shall carry out
a thorough evaluation of current agency practices
for making benefit and cost calculations and shall
publish a planning manual that will ensure that
benefits and costs are estimated using the best
current techniques and calculated accurately, consistently and in compliance with the Principles and
Standards and other applicable economic evaluation
requirements. This manual should supplement and
implement the Principles and Standards and other
applicable economic evaluation requirements.

The new benefit/cost procedures should, among other
things, eliminate double counting and inclusion of
benefits that are inconsistent with Federal policy
or sound economic rationale. Particular attention
shall be given to the following items: benefits
attributed to protecting future development in the
floodplain; surplus crop benefits; navigation benefits (including regional "savings to shippers");
flat-water recreation benefits; extended project
life; area redevelopment benefits; the appropriateness
of calculations for ability to pay (reclamation
projects); whether benefits to charter boats should
be defined as commercial navigation; uncertainty and
risk of cost and benefits; least cost alternative
analysis; consideration and display of engineering
uncertainty; market value of vendible project outputs; determination of project design flood; the
appropriateness of maximizing benefit/cost ratios
under budget constraints; the assessment and consideration of costs of elimination of farmland, wetlands, wildlife habitat, and timberland."

The general objective in completing this manual is to
produce a series of procedures which can be used by field
offices of all Federal water resource development agencies
to more adequately plan water resources management projects.
This manual will also insure consistency among agencies so
that projects planned by different agencies can be compared.

Finally, the President directed the Water Resources Council to implement a project review function to provide independent and impartial monitoring of all water projects during
preauthorization and preconstruction planning:

"I will issue an Executive Order establishing in the
Water Resources Council an independent review function
to provide an impartial monitoring of all water projects
during preauthorization and preconstruction planning to

assure compliance with the Principles and
Standards and other laws and requirements related
to the water resources project planning process.
The function shall be established as soon as pos-
sible, and should be operational in time for the
FY 1981 budget cycle."

The purpose of this independent project review is to
insure compliance by the Federal water resources development
agencies with the Principles and Standards and other laws
and requirements related to the water resources project
planning process. A major objective of this independent review function is to provide factual information on the technical adequacy of the agency report in addressing important
planning aspects such as the benefit-cost ratio, cost allocation, cost sharing arrangements, consideration of alternatives, and public participation, thereby increasing public
credibility in the planning process of water resources
projects.

In accordance with these directives, the Water Resources
Council is now in the process of revising the Principles and
Standards in order to include language specifically requiring
more adequate consideration of nonstructural measures together with, or in lieu of, nonstructural measures as a solution
to water resources problems. The revised Principles and
Standards will specifically require that a "primarily non-
structural" alternative project be developed in addition to
the presently required alternatives to maximize: (1) national
economic development, and (2) environmental quality. The revised Principles and Standards will also require agencies to
specifically consider measures to reduce future demand and
consumption of water.

Development of the Principles and Standards manual is
now a major effort at the Water Resources Council. Initially
we are concentrating on the list of areas detailed in the
Presidential directive. We are also making an effort to develop new procedures in several other areas which will significantly improve the benefit-cost analysis and water resources planning done by Federal agencies. For example, present agency procedures are being analyzed and uniform procedures are being developed for estimating national economic
development benefits from municipal and industrial water
supply benefits, irrigation, agricultural flood damage, land
stabilization, drainage, urban flood damage, inland navigation, recreation, commerical fishing and trapping, increases
in output resulting from external economies and from employ-
ing unemployed or underemployed labor resources. Common
procedures will also be developed for evaluating national

economic development costs associated with: (1) displacement of farmland, wetlands, wildlife habitat and forest land, and (2) activities to mitigate the loss of wildlife habitat.

For those areas of water resources planning where benefit-cost analysis has been traditionally applied, such as the estimation of benefits resulting from municipal and industrial water supply and irrigation development, it is a matter of analyzing the procedures currently used by the agencies, determining whether an existing agency procedure is adequate and suitable for use as a common procedure by all agencies and then, if necessary, rewriting this procedure for the manual. If an existing procedure is not adequate, a new procedure is developed.

The President's directive also requires considerable effort in various areas of benefit-cost analysis and water resources planning where procedures have not been as thoroughly developed. For example, we are analyzing the present procedures used by agencies for estimating the evaluation of costs resulting from resources required or displaced due to the construction of water resources projects. Here, for example, we are concerned with the cost of farmland, wetlands, wildlife habitat and forest land. We are also looking at ways in which the agencies estimate the costs of mitigating wildlife habitat losses. While these procedures may appear mundane, they are very important in determining whether the Nation, as a whole, is best served by developing a water resource in one manner or another, or preserving the water resource.

The existing Principles and Standards require agencies to evaluate the beneficial and adverse effects to environmental quality from proposed water resources projects. Here the procedures generally used by agencies are usually less sophisticated than those procedures for estimating economic benefits and costs. Because of existing deficiencies in the theory and practice of evaluating beneficial and adverse effects on environmental quality, considerably more effort will be required to develop common procedures for use by field level offices. The major goal here will be to establish procedures for use by field level offices which can produce consistent and verifiable estimates of environmental quality benefits and costs. Such procedures must be capable of dealing with projects and programs concerned with the protection, enhancement, or creation of open or green space, free-flowing rivers, lakes, beaches, shores, mountain and wilderness areas, estuaries, or other areas of natural beauty. The procedures must also be concerned with the preservation or enhancement of especially valuable archeologi-

cal, historical, biological and geological resources and
selected ecological systems. Finally, the procedures must be
capable of dealing with the preservation of freedom of choice
to future resource users by actions that minimize or avoid
irreversible or irretrievable action. There is nothing new
about deficiencies in procedures designed to incorporate consideration of environmental quality into decisionmaking.
What is new is an effort to develop operational procedures,
for use by field level offices, to incorporate consideration
of environmental quality in water resources development decisionmaking.

Development of operational procedures to incorporate
more adequate consideration of environmental quality into
water resources planning is only one of several efforts that
are required to improve implementation of the Principles and
Standards. Over the next two years, an effort will be made
to develop a complete set of procedures for full implementation of the Principles and Standards as detailed in the following outline. The outline will be subject to considerable
change as work progresses, but should provide a general indi-
cation of the scope and magnitude of the effort involved.

Tentative Outline of the Planning Manual

    I. Purpose
        A. Authority and Relationship to the Principles
           and Standards
        B. Agency Activities Covered by the Manual
        C. Responsibility for Application of the Manual;
           Development of Agency Procedures
        D. Schedule for Application of the Manual
        E. Modification of the Manual

   II. General
        A. General Setting
        B. Measurement of Beneficial and Adverse Effects
        C. Price Relationships
        D. The Discount or Interest Rate
        E. Consideration of Comparison of Alternatives
        F. Period of Analysis
        G. Calculation of Net Benefits
        H. Project Scaling Using Net Benefits Analysis
        I. Design Flood
        J. Dam Failure
        K. Scheduling
        L. Risk and Uncertainty
        M. Sensitivity Analysis
        N. Updating Plans

III. Procedures for Plan Formulation
    A. Objectives for Plan Formulation
        1. National Economic Development
        2. Environmental Quality
    B. Definitions
        1. Purposes as Components of Formulation
            Objectives
        2. Alternatives
        3. Evaluation Objectives
    C. Sequence of Plan Formulation Steps
        1. Identification of Water and Related Land
            Resource Purposes to be Served
        2. Projected Conditions Without the Plan
        3. Specification of Alternatives
        4. Development of NED, EQ and Nonstructural
            Plans
        5. Evaluation of Alternative Plans
        6. Reconsideration of Purposes, Levels of
            Achievement and Alternatives Considered
        7. Plan Selection
    D. Participation
    E. Tests of Final Plan
        1. Efficiency
        2. Effectiveness
        3. Completeness
        4. Acceptability
    F. Reporting Requirements
        1. Data Used
        2. Assumptions
        3. Procedures
        4. Basis for Recommended Plan

IV. Procedures for the Evaluation of NED Benefits
    A. Water Supply
        1. Municipal and Industrial Water Supply
        2. Agricultural Water Supply (Irrigation)
    B. Flood Control
        1. Agricultural Flood Damage
        2. Agricultural Drainage
        3. Urban Flood Damage
    C. Power, Hydropower
    D. Transportation, Inland Navigation
    E. Recreation
    F. Commercial Fishing and Trapping
    G. Increases in Output Resulting from External
        Economies
    H. Special Effects from Use of Unemployed or Under-
        employed Labor Resources
    I. Deepwater Navigation
    J. Beach Erosion Control
    K. National Parks and Recreation Areas

L. Wild, Scenic, Recreational Rivers and Wilderness
    Areas
M. Wetlands and Estuaries
N. Coastal Zones
O. Federal Waterfowl Refuges

V. Procedures for the Evaluation of Adverse Effects
    on National Economic Development
    A. General Procedures
        1. Measurement Methods
        2. With and Without Analysis
        3. Limitations
    B. The Protection, Enhancement or Creation of Open
        and Green Space, Wild and Scenic Rivers, Lakes,
        Beaches, Shores, Mountain and Wilderness
        Areas, Estuaries, or Other Areas of Natural
        Beauty
    C. The Preservation and Enhancement of Especially
        Valuable Archaeological, Historical, Biological,
        and Geological Resources and Selected Ecological
        Systems
    D. The Enhancement of Selected Quality Aspects of
        Water, Land and Air
    E. The Preservation of Freedom of Choice to Future
        Resource Users by Actions that Minimize or Avoid
        Irreversible or Irretrievable Effects

VII. Procedures for the Evaluation of RD Benefits and Costs
    A. General Procedures
        1. Measurement Methods
        2. With and Without Analysis
        3. Interregional Transfer
        4. Limitations
    B. Regional Income
    C. Regional Employment
    D. Population Distribution
    E. Regional Economic Base and Stability
    F. Environmental Conditions of Special Regional
        Concern

VIII. Procedures for the Evaluation of SWB Benefits and
       Costs
    A. General Procedures
        1. Measurement Methods
        2. With and Without Analysis
        3. Limitations
    B. Effects on Real Incomes
    C. Effects on Security of Life, Health and Safety
    D. Education, Cultural and Recreation Opportunities
    E. Effects on Energy Preparedness
    F. Other

IX. Cost Allocation
    A. Introduction
    B. Summary of the Cost Allocation Methods
    C. The Cost Allocation Method
        1. Cost Allocation Among Objectives
        2. Cost Allocation Among Components
           a. The National Economic Development Objectives
           b. The Environmental Quality Objective
    D. Definitions
        1. Components
        2. Alternatives
        3. Incremental Costs
        4. Separate Costs
        5. Remaining Joint Costs
    E. Application of the Cost Allocation Method
    F. Review of Cost Allocations

Independent Review Function

The Water Resources Council is also implementing the independent review function as directed by the President in E.O. 12113. This responsibility does not place veto authority in the Water Resources Council to vote a project up or down but is rather an effort to insure quality control in the planning and benefit-cost analysis performed by water resources development agencies and to increase the credibility of this analysis. The independent project review function is intended to work closely with and support the Principles and Standards. It is expected that feedback from the independent review function will be used to improve the Principles and Standards manual while minimizing delay and unnecessary requirements on the agencies.

Implementation of the independent review will require a division of responsibilities between the Office of Management and Budget and the Water Resources Council since OMB has previously conducted a technical review of proposed Federal water projects as part of their overall budget process. The Council and OMB have established the following division of responsiblities:

1. WRC will produce a statement of findings for each water project reviewed. The statement will include a factual analysis of compliance or noncompliance with the Principles and Standards, planning manual, environmental statutes and other applicable laws and regulations. The statement will provide factual information on the technical adequacy of the agency report in addressing important planning aspects such

as the benefit-cost ratio, cost allocation, cost sharing arrangements, consideration of alternatives, and public participation.

2.   Reports submitted to OMB will not be accepted unless a statement of WRC findings is included.

3.   WRC review will normally be limited to 60 days (absolute maximum of 90 days) and will replace the OMB technical review that has previously had an unknown duration.

4.   The WRC findings statement will be made available to the Congress and to the public for information on the project.

5.   The appropriate agency head will decide whether to amend or modify the project report in light of WRC findings before submittal to OMB.   The WRC review process should not be construed as veto authority on an agency project report.

6.   OMB will review: (a) authorization reports for consistency with Presidential policy, and (b) construction funding requests with regard to their consistency with Presidential policy and budget priorities.   OMB will not duplicate the WRC review of planning aspects, but will accept the WRC findings.

The WRC statement of findings will indicate the degree of compliance with the Principles and Standards and the new planning manual, and the technical adequacy of the report. Specific variations from approved planning procedures, laws, regulations and guidelines will be identified and revisions necessary to bring the plan into compliance will be de-- scribed.   Agency submissions to OMB and the Congress must be accompanied by the statement of findings.   However, an agency can:

- revise the report to comply with findings,
- ignore the findings,
- seek a compromise, or
- explain disagreement with the findings.

The review will apply to preconstruction proposals and plans (authorization and initial appropriation) covered by the Principles and Standards, including those of the Corps of Engineers, the Soil Conservation Service, Bureau of Reclamation, Tennessee Valley Authority, and other agencies.

The independent review function has been criticized as "another layer of bureaucratic review" which will further delay project implementation. In response to this, it is important to indicate that the WRC independent review function will substitute for the current substantive review function at OMB and that OMB will only retain responsibility for overall budget considerations involving water projects and will not do substantive review of water projects.

Conclusion

There has been a quick overview of the tasks now underway at the Water Resources Council to improve the analysis and planning of proposed water resources projects and insure construction of water projects in the future which are economically efficient and environmentally sound.

William C. Ackermann

4. Research Under the New Water Policy

Introduction

After about a year of effort within the federal bureau-
cracy, and with sometimes heated inputs from the States,
various interest groups, and the public, the President announced his water policy initiatives on June 6, 1978. His
initiatives have done anything but calm the waters of con-
troversy which appear to be making larger waves than ever.
The federal agencies under principal leadership of the Department of Interior have organized themselves under 19
Task Committees to carry out the President's policy.
Numerous groups including professional societies are analyzing the policy initiatives and preparing position statements, and Congress is expected to take some initiatives of
its own. Meanwhile, announcement of a major reorganization
of the federal agencies concerned with water and other
natural resources is anticipated.

Other speakers on this session will consider other
technological, institutional, and urban aspects of improving federal water resources policy and programs.

The present paper will attempt to formulate some insights into the research implications of the new water
policy. It is necessary to speak of insights and implications because in announcing his water policy initiatives
the President did not find it necessary to mention the word
research. What he did call for was:

1. Improved planning and efficient management of
    federal water resource programs to prevent waste
    and to permit necessary water projects which are
    cost effective, safe, and environmentally sound
    to move forward expeditiously;

2. Provide a new, national emphasis on water
    conservation;

3. Enhance Federal-State cooperation and improved
    State water resources planning; and

4. Increase attention to environmental quality.

One must assume that the President and his advisors
recognize that changes in policy and emphasis must necessarily require new research directions to find improved
means of achieving the desired goals. But we are left with
the task of deducing these research directions because they
are not enunciated, and probably have not received a great
deal of thought within the administration.

.In this paper it seems appropriate to recall briefly
the research needs called for during the past 15 years because many of these are unmet or only partially met. We
also will review two major inputs into the President's
recent policy initiatives, and finally examine the initiatives themselves to identify research requirements.

Research Needs Previously Identified

The last period of water resources research attention
on a national scale flowed from the report of the U.S.
Senate Select Committee on National Water Resources. In
January 1961 that Committee reported on the extent and
character of water resources activities required to meet
the water-related needs of the United States for all purposes to the years 1980 and 2000, and drew attention to the
need for a coordinated Federal scientific research program
on water. In response, the Federal Council for Science and
Technology established a Task Group on Coordinated Water
Resources Research. Their report drew particular attention
to deficiencies in education and training, to research on
groundwater (including the infiltration processes and soil-
plant-water relationships), and to socioeconomic and water
quality research.

The Federal Council also established a Federal Committee on Water Resources Research which produced a series
of annual reports on the Federal water resources research
programs for FY 1965 through 1971, and finally the combined
years of FY 1973 and 1974. This series of reports summarized the various Federal programs by agencies and by research categories. The overriding emphasis stemming from
the Senate Select Committee and carrying through the last
of these reports was on coordination. The degree of

success must be judged as modest with coordination depending largely upon program visibility and information.

One of the most ambitious undertakings of the Committee on Water Resources Research was the report "A Ten-Year Program of Federal Water Resources Research" dated February 1966, which is commonly referred to as "The Brown Book." As one views our present research circumstance he can only marvel at the wisdom and far-sightedness of this report. It is still useful today. Although the report undoubtedly had considerable impact, the degree of research program implementation, unfortunately fell far short of what was recommended and was required. Important recommendations of the Brown Book were:

1. Research on methods and criteria for water resources planning should be increased very greatly. The same is true for research on water law, and institutional arrangements for facilitating the results of more effective planning.

2. No rational approach to the water problem is possible without a good grasp of benefits and alternatives; thus research into cost allocations, cost sharing, pricing and repayment should be greatly increased.

3. Research on improved methods of waste treatment (including techniques for complete purification of sewage and industrial waste) and on methods of dealing with pollutants from diffuse sources including fertilizers and acid mine waste should be greatly expanded.

4. A program of research on methods of conserving water in industry and municipal use should be initiated at once. In particular, steps which reduce the use of water for waste carriage should be intensively studied, both as means for saving water and reducing pollution of streams and lakes.

5. Research on methods of conserving water in agriculture should be accelerated.

6. A program of research on the possible ecologic impacts of water development should be developed in order that probable impacts can be introduced in future project planning.

7. Research on the evaluation of the effect of certain
   nonwater activities on water should be undertaken.
   The most pressing problem in this category is the
   effect of urbanization and this should receive
   first priority. The research should be aimed at
   devising methods of avoiding undesirable effects.

8. Research on evaluating climatic changes and the
   significance of fluctuations from flood to drought
   should be prosecuted vigorously.

9. Careful assessment of the extent and character of
   various water-oriented problems should be a pre-
   lude to research on specific problems, and funds
   for such assessments should be a normal part of
   the research budget.

10. General assessments of the following problem areas
    should be undertaken promptly to aid the manage-
    ment of ongoing research programs:

    - The areas of potential use of sea and
      brackish water desalting techniques.

    - Potential for water-yield improvement
      through land management.

    - Potential for water conservation through
      better use of poor quality water.

    - The sources, quantities and characteristics
      of pollutants in U.S. water sources.

    - Potential water recovery through waste
      water purification.

    - The Committee recognizes the possible
      future impact of precipitation modifica-
      tion on water resources.

11. A review in depth of the current Federal program
    of experimental watersheds is recommended. The
    review should attempt to define the appropriate
    scope for such a program, determine the feasi-
    bility of consolidating activities at selected
    experimental areas, consider the possibility that
    some existing sites may be discontinued, and ar-
    range for the prompt publication of data for the
    use of all research workers.

12. In view of the rapidly expanding needs for intensive and comprehensive water resources development, research aimed at increasing the efficacy and at reducing the huge and mounting costs of engineering works of unprecedented magnitude and complexity must be strengthened promptly.

The Committee on Water Resources Research which authored the Brown Book suffered a nearly fatal blow when President Nixon terminated the Office of Science and Technology as an activity of the Executive Office, and the Committee function was relegated to the Department of Interior. Its last effort, so far as I know, was a report "Directions in U.S. Water Research: 1978-1982" which was not published.

Another comprehensive examination of water research was prepared by the Universities Council on Water Resources for the Office of Water Resources Research, Department of the Interior Circa 1972. Dr. Warren Viessman, Jr., then Director of the Water Resources Research Institute for Nebraska, was the Principal Investigator.

This excellent report was organized according to (1) Water Research and Social Goals, (2) Major Water Research Problems, (3) Research Areas-Classification and Emphasis, and (4) Research Management. The report dealt with substantive research areas and rated these as to their degree of urgency. It was unique in that it identified for the first time two additional research areas: (1) Ecological Response to Water Development and (2) Human Behavior and Institutions. These are particularly significant in the light of the new directions called for in the President's initiatives.

Unfortunately the report was caught up in the period of declining water research fortunes during the Nixon administration, and so far as this author knows, never was printed or made widely available.

One could cite various other studies, events and activities related to water resources research in the decade and one-half since the Senate Select Committee report. In my view, one of the brightest and most productive was the Water Resources Research Act of 1964 (PL 88-379). This Act created the Office of Water Resources Research (OWRR), which later became the Office of Water Research and Technology (OWRT) in the Department of Interior. This program raised extramural water research by an order of magnitude, and essentially solved one of the originally identified needs --

training and education. It is hoped that this program will
be continued.

Reports Prepared for the President's Initiative

Moving now to more recent times, I would like to
mention two reports which were prepared as inputs to the
President's policy study. The first of these was entitled
"Report of the Water Resources Research Task Force, National
Water Policy Study," dated November 30, 1977. Although the
findings of this report unfortunately were not given any
apparent visibility in the President's announced policy
initiatives, its content is valuable in our considerations
here today. In the introduction an overview statement said
in part:

> "The President has expressed concern over
> our priorities in dealing with the Nation's water
> resources. Consequently, he has ordered a policy
> study to be made for the purpose of examining
> and reordering our national priorities, responsi-
> bilities, and procedures in national water manage-
> ment. Such reordering cannot stand for all time,
> but must remain flexible to natural and social
> change and to refinements. Such refinements will
> come in large measure from adequate data and the
> findings of a balanced, timely, and efficient
> research program. Thus, our national water re-
> search program must be viable, responsive to
> many and varied needs; and its products must be
> available to decision makers and the public.

> "Water research has not received substantial
> attention since 1962-64. The research system put
> in place at that time has had its mandate eroded
> and national attention diminished. It is impera-
> tive that research be given a new and broadened
> national charter so as to provide the needed
> leadership and coordination that would make it
> possible for the policy initiatives of the
> President to be carried out."

The report of the Water Resources Research Task Force
attempts to develop the process whereby the research needs
of the Nation can be focused upon and met and knowledge put
to use in the management of our water resources.

The Task Force report also identifies a number of important areas of research which have not been adequately

addressed. Substantive areas in need of strengthening are:

1. Urban water research

2. Energy-related water research

3. Water reuse research and development

4. Desalting research and development

5. Drought research
.

6. Groundwater research

7. Water conservation research

8. Environmental protection research

9. Rural water research

A second important input to the President's water resources policy study originated in the Office of Science and
Technology Policy and was entitled "Scientific and Technological Aspects of Water Resources Policy" dated January 19,
1978. The report in somewhat modified form was published
in the June 1978 issue of EOS, The Transactions of the
American Geophysical Union. Our session chairman, Dr. Yacov
Y. Haimes, was the individual who directed this OSTP effort.
Because of the ready availability of the EOS article, and
because Dr. Haimes may himself draw upon that report in the
session today, the briefest summary is attempted here. The
report identifies problem areas which are analyzed with respect to: (1) issue definition, (2) findings, (3) policy
recommendations, and (4) research directions. The areas of
consideration are:

1. Climate and water supply

2. Floods

3. Droughts

4. Groundwater and its conjunctive use with surface
   water

5. Water conservation in irrigation

6. Water quality

7. Erosion and sedimentation

8. Water for energy

9. New methods to increase water supply

10. Future demands for water

11. Other issues, including urban water programs, and a systems approach for water

With respect to research directions the OSTP report points out that our understanding of the physical, chemical, biological, economic, and social aspects of water resources has grown rapidly. However, one result of our changing perception of the water problem is the need to identify important gaps which remain in our current knowledge and the need, at times, to rework old fields of knowledge. For example, measures of efficiency in irrigation water use were designed to provide guidelines for maximum crop response and give little guidance for conserving water. Or, we know a lot about how plants respond to nutrients that are added to the soil, but not much about the fate of the nutrients that the plants did not take up, and which now add to the pollution burden. Thus, where current knowledge is inadequate to guide decisions in areas of today's problems, further research is required.

The Water Resources Policy Study: An Assessment

This report by Dr. Warren Viessman, Jr., Senior Specialist in Engineering and Public Works for the Congressional Research Service, Publication No. 95-108, was issued in June 1978, at about the same time as the President's initiatives. It is a comprehensive review of water resources policy. On the subject of research Dr. Viessman said:

> "President Carter's emphasis on improved water management strongly supports a dynamic and responsive water research program, one that considers the nature of both current and emerging problems. The water policy study stresses problems of coordination, prioritization, and technology transfer, but fails to consider, or is not explicit on companion issues . . . ."

He goes on to mention the absence of guidance on research funding, manpower training, and the mix of pure

versus applied research. Dr. Viessman then discusses alternative institutional arrangements, but does not attempt to
identify substantive research areas.

Research Implications of the President's
Water Policy Initiatives

There seems little doubt that much of the President's
policy initiatives can be put in place by executive order,
by changes in agency regulations and procedures, or by
legislation. In this broad category we would place uniform
application for estimating benefits and costs. Here, also,
is the safety review and modification of existing structures such as dams, and the requirement to consider environmental values. Alternative non-structural plans can be required. Independent review of projects to insure conform-
ance with criteria can be required if a governmental loca-
tion for this can be found which is satisfactory to
Congress and is not sabotaged by the Federal agencies.
Priorities for project implementation can be assigned which
are consistent with the cost sharing and economic principles
outlined.

Funding is a second powerful approach which can be
employed by the President and the Congress to manage water
resources. Included here is the reassessment and highly
selective funding of the $34 billion backlog of water pro-
jects which are either authorized or under construction.
Here, also, is the President's intention to retain juris-
diction in State government for planning and management of
water resources. I believe that his proposed planning
grants to the States will be effective in stimulating the
States in carrying out these responsibilities.

Resolution of the Indian water rights and reserved
Federal rights are important issues in the West, and in a
special category which certainly must be resolved promptly.

There are, however, three areas attractive for research related to the President's initiatives, although he
certainly does not explicitly call for such research. These
three topics are treated in the following sections.

Incentives for water conservation. The most prominent
theme in the President's initiatives is the call for a conservation ethic. It is consistent with his desire to reduce expenditures and to meet water needs by attention to
demand management while limiting supply enlargement.

We hope that conservation will be interpreted as more
than reducing water use, but rather be considered the efficient management of water resources. Important opportunities exist for water conservation in agriculture,
domestic use, and industry. Although much technology exists
in these and other areas, and incrementally improved technology can result from further research, we wish to
emphasize research on incentives which will result in the
implementation of presently known technology.

It is believed that the greatest opportunities for
improved water management exist in the socioeconomic, institutional, and political areas. Here a broad and diverse
research program is required on problems such as design and
evaluation of institutions for redistributing water resources into alternative uses through more efficient use of
existing facilities, joint management of water supply and
waste water systems, regionalization of water systems, the
functioning of policy-making institutions and processes that
encourage water conservation, the impact of the behavior of
organizations and individuals on the public and individual
perceptions of water conservation, and the importance of
water management tools such as pricing, subsidies, information dissemination, regulations, and other incentives and
disincentives for water conservation. Specific examples
might include research on systems for marketing water rights,
behavioral response to changes in water pricing, case
studies of responses to drought or to changes in water
pricing and other incentives for adoption of water conserving technology.

In summary, with regard to water conservation research
it is believed that worthwhile and incremental improvements
can result through research in the physical and biological
aspects of water technology, but the large and important
research is in the social sciences, leading to what may
broadly be classed as incentives for water conservation.

In-stream water use. Along with conservation one of
the strong themes of the President's water policy initiatives is his emphasis on in-stream water uses, and particularly in reference to environmental values and fish and
wildlife. To quote from his message he says at various
places, for example:

"Some water projects . . . have caused
losses of natural streams and rivers, fish and
wildlife habitat and recreational opportunities."

"Funding for mitigation of fish and wildlife damages should be provided concurrently and proportionately with construction funding."

"I am particularly concerned about the need to improve the protection of instream flows . . ."

"I also call upon the Governors and the Congress to work with the Federal agencies to protect the fish and wildlife and other values associated with adequate instream flows. New and existing projects should be planned and operated to protect instream flows, consistent with State law and in close consultation with States. Where prior commitments and economic feasibility permit, amendments to authorizing statutes should be sought in order to provide for streamflow maintenance."

"Together we can protect and manage our nation's water resources . . . preserving our rivers and streams for future generations."

Some might consider this heavy emphasis to be an instream overkill. It might also be viewed with some concern by interests who presently utilize our streams for navigation, power plant cooling purposes, or off-stream uses for public water supply and irrigation.

In any case, this heavy and broad emphasis on environmental values and aquatic life calls for assessments and allocations of use which will touch all aspects of water resources. Certainly research must loom large if wise public decisions are to be made in the allocation of stream uses. While existing uses are subject to reasonably accurate evaluations and projections, the requirements of living organisms in the extremely complicated ecological chains of our streams and lakes are poorly understood. So the legitimate requirements of aquatic life need to be established through research before such uses and attendant water allocations and trade-offs can be made by our political system. Thus, this author finds the need for a greatly accelerated program of ecologically related research to properly implement the President's initiatives in this area.

Land use - stream flow research. A major area of hydrologic/hydraulic research needs to be regenerated in this country in light of the recognized environmental problems and the President's initiatives. One important aspect of such a research program is in the urban setting,

and it is assumed that this will be addressed by Mr. Ray
Kudukis, another speaker on this symposium. In light of
that assumption, my remarks will be addressed to the non-
urban sector.

Some 40 years ago the U.S. had in place an extensive
program of experimental watersheds which was aimed at obtaining information on the effect of agricultural and
forestry practices on streamflow. Such watersheds were
operated primarily by the Agricultural Research Service and
the Forest Service for the guidance of the Soil Conservation Service and other operating agencies. The value of
this experimental network has now largely been exploited,
and many of the watersheds have been abandoned.

The watersheds of a generation ago were primarily concerned with agricultural and forestry practices in vogue at
that time. The watershed studies were also concerned primarily with the quantitative aspects of surface water.
Little information was obtained on groundwater, soil
moisture, or on water quality - including sediment yield -
all of which are of great interest today.

It is not within the scope of this paper to outline in
detail the nature of a presently needed experimental watershed program beyond its general dimensions. However, to
sample the diverse soils, climates, and land uses will
probably require at least 100 watersheds which must be con-
trolled through purchase, lease, or designation of public
lands. We are also speaking of extensive instrumentation
and research and supportive staff. The cost will be in the
order of $10,000,000 per year for 20 years.

To mount such a program in the governmental and funding
climate of today will take a concerted effort by the
agencies and interests which are concerned with wise land
use, the environment, and pollution from non-point sources.
It is certainly basic to programs for stream and groundwater
quality and quantity and to controlling our appalling
erosion and sedimentation.

In summary, our history of water resources research of
the past 20-40 years is paved with the good intentions of
thoughtful studies of research needs which have been only
partially fulfilled. Meanwhile, important parts of our research apparatus of the past have fallen into disuse and
obsolescence. New needs in the areas of the environment,
water quality, and groundwater - recently capped by the
President's initiatives - makes urgent that a new generation
of hydrologic research be initiated.

5. Institutional Aspects of National Water Policy

Abstract

This paper presents the thesis that the development and implementation of an explicit national water policy is hampered by the lack of institutions, at all levels of government, with the authority to coordinate such efforts to produce a balanced, considerate, comprehensive view of water problems and their possible solutions. This situation is made more severe by the general lack of formal linkages between existing agencies having responsibility for various aspects of water policy development or implementation.

The historical development of this problem is discussed, and the present water resources institutional situation in the United States is outlined. Suggestions for making certain institutional changes in the system are offered, and the importance of this subject to the scientific community is explored.

Introduction

Historical Development

In the spring of 1977 President Carter announced as a goal for his new Administration the development of a comprehensive, coordinated, and explicit national water policy. This initiative reflected the President's awareness of the changes that the last 50 years have wrought in this Nation's concepts of the goals and values of natural resources management.

This concern with water policy, although admirable, is not unique, as almost every administration in the past 100 years has addressed this issue. Most often this has taken

the form of a Presidential Commission or Task Force assigned
to study national water policy needs. Unfortunately, the
results of such efforts have largely included recommendations
that demanded high, often prohibitive, political costs for
their implementation. Thus, although the matter has been
throughly studied for years, little has been done towards
articulation of, or, implementation of a comprehensive national policy on water resources management.

In one respect the Carter approach has been decidedly
different. Rather than appoint another study commission,
he directed his Administration to seek assistance from the
States and the public at large in examining the countless
recommendations made by past national water policy studies
and to use these materials in the development of a comprehensive policy.

Current Expression

In June of 1978, more than a year after he announced his
intention in this regard, the President presented his Federal
water policy initiatives to the Congress. In this statement
he emphasized four key areas, i.e.,

- improved planning and efficient management of
  Federal water resource programs;

- a new national emphasis on water conservation;

- enhanced Federal-State cooperation and improved
  State water resources planning; and

- increased attention to environmental quality.

Several program elements, designed to translate these
broad policy considerations into effective programs have
been addressed by the Administration since that time. Some
of these require new legislation, some require new regulations under existing authority, while others require administrative changes only. Still others require only the report-
ing of data, the establishment of new working relationships
or the adoption of new strategies towards the solution of
old problems. Proposed changes which have elicited the most
discussion include those to strengthen the U.S. Water Resources Council by having it undertake the development of
(i) a uniform planning methodology for Federal planning and
construction agencies, (ii) revised principles and standards
for water resources planning, and (iii) an independent technical review of all Federal agency proposed water projects

and programs. Also of great interest is proposed legislation which would (i) increase funding to States for programs in water planning and water conservation, and (ii) change the rules of Federal-State cost-sharing on water projects.

It must be recognized that U.S. water policy development and implementation is of necessity multifaceted and diverse in nature. The Administration attempted to deal with this complexity by the establishment of Federal task forces dealing with each of the major areas of Presidential concern. These task forces function under the overall policy guidance of the Secretary of the Interior.

Efforts in this respect have been intense. However, after two years of task force deliberations, numerous public meetings, press releases, conferences and related activities, there is still a great lack of understanding, or agreement, throughout the country over what the Administration is trying to do vis-a-vis water policy. This may be true in part because the goals and objectives of such a policy, and their relationships to other national goals and objectives continue to be vague. In fact, a clear, concise expression of the Administration's interest in water policy, of how all the many bits and pieces of this interest fit together into a whole, and of how water policy relates to other national interests continues to be missing. Perhaps because of such deficiencies, many continue to regard these efforts as related to *Federal* rather than a *national* water policy.

Of course, it is reasonable, perhaps even necessary, to begin the process with an examination of Federal policy and programs. And, as debate continues, input from other levels of government and the many and varied interest groups will undoubtedly begin to give the policy consideration a more truly national flavor. This process, however, has been crippled from the beginning by an unrealistic time frame, which has mitigated against calm, reasonable debate on the issues, and that has contributed to misunderstanding of and/or disagreement with the President's proposals.

In spite of such problems, current Administration efforts in this respect represent perhaps the strongest start ever made toward the development and implementation of an explicit, comprehensive, water policy adequate to this Nation's present and future needs. They have also brought to light, however, glaring deficiencies in the Nation's ability to deal with water and related resource management; i.e., the lack, at all levels of government, of appropriate institutions for dealing with such questions in a coordinated, comprehensive fashion, and the lack of adequate linkages in this respect between existing institutions.

U.S. Institutional Expression of Water Policy

Background

The institutional deficiencies mentioned above result from the piecemeal approach to water management which has been traditional in the United States. Over the past 200 years this country, in response to various perceived needs, has developed a multitude of institutions to deal with various facets of the water resources management effort, each with a rather narrowly defined mission. For example, early efforts in water resources management centered around the taming and development of rivers and streams for economic purposes, such as power production and navigation, and the development of ports and harbors. Urbanization and westward expansion led to a recognition of the need for flood control measures; for dams, levies, bridges, and channelization projects. In the early part of this century the Congress made it a part of national policy to develop and utilize the water resources of our western States for agriculture to promote industry, commerce, and settlement of the region.

The institutions created to meet such expressed needs-- the Corps of Engineers, the Bureau of Reclamation, the Soil Conservation Service, the Tennessee Valley Authority, and others--have for the most part done their jobs quite well and this country has excelled in the management of its waters for navigation, for power production, for irrigation, for urban water supplies, and in the control of flooding.

As the country matured, however, recognition began to be given to other important uses of water and public discussion began to include what has been termed the "amenity" values of water; for example, those values that are associated with recreational, fish and wildlife, scenic, and water quality uses. Following the traditional pattern of governmental response in the United States, new institutions were created to deal with these new concerns and values. The National Environmental Policy Act authorized creation of the Environmental Protection Agency and the Council on Environmental Quality. The older Fish and Wildlife Service was given a new mission in the implementation of the Endangered Species Act. These agencies, and others similar to them, were designed to define and express these new values, and to help insure that they are given full considerations along with the older, more traditional economic values in the making of water resources decisions.

This proliferation of agencies authorized to deal with some particular aspect of a single problem or set of problems has created for this country a most perplexing dilemma in resource management. Because the new values often conflict directly with the older ones, the missions of these new agencies often conflict directly with the missions of the older ones; and, we have failed to develop adequate means, short of expensive, time-consuming litigation for bringing these agencies, and the values which they represent, together for achieving effective compromise and acceptable solutions to the conflicts so produced.

In part, past failure in this respect can be attributed to the lack of a well defined national policy on water resources management. It is exceedingly difficult to achieve effective compromise in water management activities in the absence of an overall, explicit policy. Thus, the current Administration already has played a major role in this conflicting resolution by simply beginning the process of defining national water policy.

The Current Situation

Little attention has been given to the many problems arising out of the multiplicity of institutions that have been created to deal with the management of water and related resources. For example, at the Federal level alone, there are more than thirty--no one is really sure how many--major agencies dealing with water resources research, education, planning, program implementation, and overview. Of course, in the Congress there are several subcommittees, in both Houses, that have authority over these agencies and/or their budgets.

At the regional level there are a variety of institutions dealing with water including river basin commissions, interstate compact agencies, several interagency coordinating committees, and the regional economic assistance commissions.

In each of the fifty States there is at least one major water agency, and most States have water management functions relegated to several different agencies. For example, in Nebraska there are nine major State agencies with important functions in water planning and management.

At the local level there are uncounted numbers of agencies related to this effort, some directly and some indirectly. These include water supply and wastewater control districts, natural resource districts, county planning and water agencies, city planning and water agencies, irrigation districts, rural water districts, and conservation districts.

At present, these agencies act largely on their own, and their activities relate primarily to a very narrow set of interests. There is little in the way of agencies or agency authority for providing overall policy direction to these activities; for assuring at all levels of government a balanced, considerate, comprehensive view of water problems and their possible solutions.

Furthermore, formal direct linkages between coordinating bodies, where they exist, and the various agencies--imperative to the coordinated implementation of water policy and to the coordination of water policy with other areas of national policy--are practically nonexistent.

Federal

At the Federal level the major water coordinating body is the U.S. Water Resources Council, which is responsible for coordination of the major Federal water agencies, including those of the Departments of Agriculture, Army, Commerce, Energy, Housing and Urban Development, Interior, Transportation, and the Environmental Protection Agency. By law, the Council and its staff also are concerned with the assessment of the Nation's water problems and with the preplanning efforts needed to define alternatives for solving these problems.

Since its beginning, the Council has been under constant criticism and attack from almost every quarter. It poses something of a threat to the prerogatives of the member agencies, especially as its Chairman is the head of one of these agencies (Interior); it has often served as a focal point for battles between the Executive Branch and the Congress over water policy and its implementation; it has no mechanism for receiving formal advice from the States, which theoretically and legally control most of this Nation's water resources; its staff has tended to emphasize its water assessment, preplanning, rule-making, and review roles more than its coordination role; and its mission is little understood or appreciated by most of the country's water related special interest groups. It has not received firm marching orders from either the Congress or the Executive Branch; it has not been assigned sufficient funds for the development of an adequate staff; and the authority of its Director and, indeed, of the Council itself, has been lacking. Initially, water quality management, a major water management effort in this country in terms of overall expenditures, was not even a consideration of the Council. Even today, the water planning efforts of the Environmental Protection Agency are largely outside of the Council's purview. All of this is somewhat regretable, as the basic idea of a coordinating Council for the major Federal water agencies is a sound one, addressing an important need.

The present Administration has taken a hard look at the Council and has devoted considerable effort to strengthening it. Currently, the major Federal agencies seem to be giving higher consideration and priority to the functioning of the Council, and in large measure this has generated a more active policy input to its deliberations. Additional administrative initiatives in this regard include directives giving it responsibilities, as mentioned earlier, including revision of the principles and standards for water resources development, the development of a water resources planning manual and the development of an independent review function for water resources projects.

For the past two years, there has been a growing debate in Congress, and between Congress and the Administration, concerning the role, function, and future of the Council. This debate includes proposals for an independent Chairman or an independent board of directors to oversee the functioning of the Council and its staff. Also included are proposals that would facilitate more direct State participation in the Council's deliberations and decisions. It appears quite probable that some of these proposals for changes in the Council soon will be adopted by the Congress. It is to be hoped, however, that such changes will improve the overall coordinative function of the Council, as this function is sorely needed at the Federal level.

Regional

The Water Resources Planning Act of 1965 addressed the problems of State-Federal and State-State coordination in water management efforts, and authorized the creation of river basin commissions throughout the Nation to serve as the principal agents of such action. To date six such commissions have been formed, representing a total of thirty-two States. For the most part, these States represent the northern tier of this country, including those States of New

England, the Ohio Basin, the Great Lakes Basin, the Missouri Basin, the Upper Mississippi Basin, and the Pacific Northwest. Unfortunately, the southern and western States largely have resisted efforts toward coordination in this way. This general lack of coverage of the United States by river basin commissions has been a major problem in terms of coordination of State-Federal activities and State-State activities at the regional level.

River basin commissions are charged in the Water Resources Planning Act to:

- serve as the principal agency for the coordination of Federal, State, interstate, local and nongovernmental plans for the development of water and related land resources in its area;

- prepare and keep up to date, to the extent practicable, a comprehensive, coordinated, joint plan for Federal, State, interstate, local and nongovernmental development of water and related resources;

- recommend long-range schedules of priorities for the collection and analysis of basic data and for investigation, planning, and construction of projects; and

- foster and undertake such studies of water and related land resources problems in its area as are necessary in the preparation of the comprehensive plan.

The commission mechanism provides opportunity for a State-Federal partnership in water resources planning and coordination not otherwise available. Each commission employs a small staff to aid in the conduct of its programs and activities. The commissions meet regularly to review work and to coordinate activities of State and Federal members. Funds required for commission planning and coordination activities are provided from both State and Federal sources on a shared basis.

Over the years since their creation, these commissions have made significant progress toward developing and analyzing the basic information required for understanding, expressing, and dealing with the State, regional, and national water and related resource situations. They have developed comprehensive regional water management plans and processes for continual updating of these plans. They have developed a process for setting priorities on the water programs and projects needed for implementing these plans. And, they have initiated and conducted special studies of various types, which, among other things, have led to improved understanding of emerging issues and opportunities in water management.

However, lack of Federal support in terms of authority and resources for such efforts, and attention to them, has also been a problem. For example, in the 15 years since passage of the Act, the authorized level of Federal expenditures for the general operation of the commissions has remained the same. In addition, although the Chairman of each river basin commission is a Presidential appointee, there has been little effort on the part of the White House to maintain clear and regular communication with the commissions. The Congress, also, has shown little knowledge of, or interest in the Commissions. Thus, a fundamental requirement for the success of a commission's activities--the ability to be heard by policy makers and program designers at the national level-- has been largely missing.

Furthermore, in many cases, State support of existing river basin commissions is inadequate in terms of their relinquishing either authority or assigning fiscal and human resources to commission activities. For example, the Federal Act requires all of the river basin commissions to proceed by concensus, however, concensus is defined in different ways among the various commissions. To some, it means complete lack of dissent by member agencies. Where this is the case, it is extremely difficult for the commissions to deal with significant problems in the face of a single State objection. In other cases, State participation in commission activities is largely proforma, and conducted by persons far removed from the active machinery of State policy making.

State and Local

Although some very good examples can be found of water management coordinating mechanisms at the State and local level, efforts in this regard for most areas of the United States are inadequate or nonexistent. Few State or local governments give a high priority to such activity, most State and local decision makers preferring to see "action" rather than study and deliberation. There are examples, however, wherein State government has taken the lead in developing both a State level coordinating mechanism and in linking it to a local coordinating mechanism. Nebraska presents one such model of this approach, although its efforts in this respect are so new that it is difficult to assess its effectiveness.

In the early seventies, Nebraska developed a statewide water and related resource planning and management system. The system consists of local institutions--Natural Resources Districts--organized largely along hydrologic basin lines, and covering the entire State. The Districts are managed by locally elected officials and they have rather broad powers, including that of taxation. The Districts are linked to State government through a Natural Resources Commission, composed of a representative from each District, and three gubernatorial appointees. This body is linked to regional and national water management activities through appointment of its Executive Director as a Nebraska representative to the Missouri River Basin Commission.

Nebraska recently has taken a further positive step toward coordination of its total interests in water management. Through joint legislative and gubernatorial action, a Governor's Interagency Water Coordinating Committee has been formed; chaired by the Governor and further composed of the heads of the State agencies having significant interest in water management, this body will coordinate the States' overall water planning and program review activities. This action also established a Public Advisory Board to advise the Governor and agency officials of public concerns regarding the management and use of Nebraska water resources.

Hopefully, the Nebraska system will be successful in linking and coordinating efforts of the myriad disparate entities responsible for some component of water management within its borders.

Prognosis

In spite of the multitude of water planning and management agencies across the country, however, and the lack of linkages between these, and between them and the various policy making individuals or bodies, coordination of effort does occur to some degree. For example, in those areas covered by river basin commissions coordinated comprehensive plans have been developed for the management of water and related resources through the efforts of local, State, and Federal agencies operating in the region. From these planning efforts have come priority lists for annual water management activities. The Federal government has recently given increased emphasis to the coordinating process through its declaration--by Executive Order and by a Water Resources Council policy statement--that new proposals for Federal or federally assisted water management activities must meet the test of being a part of an approved regional plan or as a part of approved regional planning objectives. This policy statement has been long overdue and demands, for successful implementation, strong State and regional capabilities in water planning and equally strong entities for creating comprehensive, regional plans out of the diversity of plans developed by the individual States.

But, as local and State interests in water resources management continue to increase and as States refine plans for managing their water resources, there will be an increasing need at the State, regional, and national levels for institutional mechanisms by which conflicts that are likely to arise between States over proposed usages of water can be identified and resolved amicably, and to assure that regional and national considerations are balanced against State and local concerns.

There are two general ways by which such needs might be adequately met, i.e., (i) by fortifying existing institutions--perhaps by formalizing their authority to a greater extent, by adding to this authority, by providing more visible linkages between them, and by increasing their resource base, and (ii) by the development of new institutions and new institutional linkages.

The probability of Federal action with regard to the reorganization or consolidation of existing water agencies into a new "super" all-inclusive water agency with a higher degree of authority and a larger budget appears to be quite small. Both the Nixon and Carter administrations have examined this possibility and considered it to be too costly in terms of political considerations. Likewise, there appears to be little enthusiam on the part of either the Administration or Congress for development of additional new agencies for dealing with the Nation's water problems.

Most likely, therefore, any institutional changes that occur in the foreseeable future will occur as changes in the structure and authority of existing entities. There are hopeful signs in this direction at the Federal level as has been mentioned above with respect to the Water Resources Council. Perhaps the Administration's proposed increase in Federal assistance to States for water planning efforts will be useful in helping them to either strengthen their existing water management institutions or formulate appropriate ones. However, to date, Federal and State concerns in this respect have largely omitted consideration for strengthening of such interstate bodies, river basin commissions, or to extending the coordinative mechanism offered by these commissions to other areas of the Nation.

The Role of the Scientific Community

The scientific community has been a part of the United States water resources planning and management effort for many years. Members of this community serve as advisors and consultants to many of the Nation's water agencies and through its research and educational activities it provides the informational and manpower base so necessary to successful implementation of national water policy.

For these reasons the scientific community should and must be a part of the debate over national water policy and the institutions by which it is to be implemented. It is the scientific community that must assure that appropriate linkages are made between efforts in water resources management; for example, between water quality and water quantity planning, between planning for the management of surface waters and ground waters, between water resource research, water resource planning, and water resource implementation, and between water resource management and other sectors of national concern, such as agricultural production, energy production, transportation, and the environment. Such linkages will not occur naturally at any level of government because of our traditional propensity for dealing with such problems in a segmented fashion; a propensity which itself has been institutionalized in the committee structure of the Congress and in State legislatures, as well as within the Federal and State bureaucracies.

Moreover, as the Nation's institutional problems in water resource management are resolved, it will become more obvious that we have water management needs beyond the institutional ones; needs which are not being met adequately. For example, if the President's concerns with regard to water conservation and protection of the environment are to be met with an adequate response, we will need to develop new water management technologies as well as new institutions. The development of both of these, of course, has in this country traditionally been the function of the academic and scientific communities. However, their development in timely fashion in this case will depend upon a greatly improved flow of monies into research and technology development areas, into overall planning efforts, and especially into the training of skilled water resource scientists and engineers.

The scientific community must contribute to effecting these desirable changes in water management institutions and program priorities, through continued efforts at elucidating

this Nation's resource management problems, and through continued dialogue with policy makers, and the public, regarding
solutions to such problems.

Conclusion

This Nation has managed during the past 100 years to
solve to a great extent many of its water resources problems.
It has navigable rivers, effective flood control programs,
large cities with adequate water supply and wastewater disposal, and large-scale irrigation for the production of food
and fiber. But, in solving these problems it has encountered
new problems and new values. It is only now learning to
respond to these new problems and values, but it is learning.
A day will come when we will be able to accommodate both the
old and new values in our approach to resource management.
However, effective, functioning coordinative bodies like the
U.S. Water Resources Council and the river basin commissions
will be necessary in order for this to occur in an efficient,
nonlitigative way. The scientific community must play a role
in seeing that such institutions are created, nurtured, and
provided with the proper mission, information, manpower, and
fiscal resources. Such institutions will, in turn, make it
easier to prove the case for increased national priorities in
water resources research and education.

6. Specific Urban Aspects of Water Resources Policy

Any discussion of water resources deals with a system which is both broad and complex, and water--as a precious natural resource and as part of an integral U.S. socio-political policy issue--must be considered in the context of a total system. In a broad examination of water use and its multiple effects (e.g., flooding, erosion, sedimentation; economic matrices; energy production and management), not only the traditional hydrological cycle but also the limited and specific aspects of water resource systems need to be addressed.

While any resource analysis must (and rightfully so) take into account household need and supply, total water resource management should bridge the entire domain of existing urban systems, including ground and surface water, and the related spectrum of wastewater treatment, disposal, and recovery. In short, commonalities among these interconnected topics must be interwoven within any national water policy.

It is understandable that any water policy intended to exercise arbitrary authority over a country as pluralistic in background and diverse in geography as the United States may create problems while solving others. Sound policy, however, is written and implemented primarily as a problem-solving tool and must be developed in that context.

With reference to a national policy on water resources, and in the specific context of President Carter's policy on conservation, it should be noted that 75 percent of the citizens of the United States reside in metropolitan communities (which have existing water-supply systems). Thus any water resources policy must focus primarily on problems emanating from existing water-supply systems. That prudent management and use of resources are mandatory and that incentives to the public and to industry for resource conservation are

essential are matters not at all at issue. The critical
issues of resource management evolve when policy becomes
unilateral, or in areas where insufficient research leads to
policies which precipitate socio-economic hardship. One
salient example articulates this policy problem:

Subsequent to the President's message on conservation,
EPA sought to amend Public Law 92-500 to require a 15 percent
reduction in water use, wherein offenders faced a reduction
in federal funding of wastewater treatment projects from 75
percent to 70 percent. Such a proposal generated extremely
negative reactions and resulted in adverse perceptions of the
whole notion of conservation.

While this particular proposal now appears to be shelved,
President Carter's June 1978 statement on conservation neither
qualified and limited nor geographically directed this conservation effort. Thus, both ambiguity in policy and the question of implementation through bureaucratic processes remain.
Undoubtedly, conservation is essential in areas of water
shortage; however, imposing arbitrary cutbacks in areas of
adequate water supply will not only spur negative effects but
are unnecessary.

Consider the Great Lakes region. While examining the
region northeast of Lake Ontario and an area from Maine to
Virginia, we can foresee water shortages in the next forty
years. (See the article by Major General James A. Johnson,
Div. Engineer, U.S. Army Corps of Engineers, "Study Predicts
Future Water Shortage for Northeast and Mid-Atlantic States,"
which appeared in Water and Sewage Works, June 1978). An expansion of the water supply system, as well as conservation
in this area, is appropriate. However, as we look to Ohio and
west, we do not see similar problems. What we do see are
cities like Cleveland, Detroit, Chicago--cities that have
existing water treatment and distribution systems. In many
areas, the systems have been paid for; are sized in terms of
needed treatment and capacity, and they generate their entire
revenue by charging for units of water consumed by their
respective customers. (In areas where this is not yet the
case, the policy will soon be the same.) The existing systems
finance improvements and expansions by sale of bonds, based
on revenues collected.

Assuming that some arbitrary (e.g., 15%) usage reduction
were imposed, the systems that are metered would experience a
15 percent reduction in revenues. The net result is an increase in rates to make up for lost revenue. Thus, in addition to the normal rate increases that emerge with rising
costs, another incremental increase would be added which would
be due solely to government policy. If we view this case in

the light of its cost-effectiveness, we find a real inconsistency: Residential and industrial customers are required to
make expenditures for new fixtures, devices and systems--all
aimed at conservation. After these payments are made, the
result is an increase in their water rates. Thus, not only
do customers pay more per unit of water used; they also have
been subjected to additional capital expenditure costs.

It is imperative that any program designed to promote
conservation must have, as its basic incentive, the goal that
reduced usage by a consumer will save money. However, for
reasons outlined above, it is obvious that, when dealing with
an existing system, the price of water to the user must be
raised to compensate for the revenue loss--but now conservation is promoted by promising the consumer some economic benefits which are basically a savings in terms of water cost.
Then when the program is implemented and usage is reduced,
the customer finds that his rates have been raised to ensure
that enough revenue is generated to properly run the system.
The net effect is not only higher prices but also depreciated
government credibility.

Another unfortunate side effect is that the utilities'
requests for future rate increases must be delayed. As a
result, the capital raised by rate increase, which, of course,
allows for the sale of bonds, is not available, and expansion
or improvement of the system must also be postponed.

Still another conflict arises with some of the basic
premises of planning. If we assume that growth eventually and
necessarily occurs, wise planning would dictate that growth
occur in areas where all necessary support systems, including
water supply, are adequate and available. If growth occurs
in regions where inadequate water supply exists, then the existing system must be expanded or new sources of supply developed. Under this policy, the limitations imposed on acquiring
new capital assuredly restrict either of the above alternatives. Another consideration, often reflected in discussions
of water conservation, is that conservation results in a de-
crease in the size of wastewater treatment plants. In the
instance where new communities and new treatment plants are
constructed, this may well be true. However, information obtained from SSES (sewer system evaluation survey) and I/I
(inflow/infiltration) studies indicates that water consumption
for sanitary purposes is not excessive.

Nonetheless, in assessing existing systems in urban
areas which have both treatment and collection systems, we
find that this type of a reduction has no bearing on the size
of a wastewater treatment plant. The main reason is that

these areas usually have combined sewer systems. The design
or upgrading of a wastewater treatment plant is or should be
dictated by EPA to be the most cost-effective possible. The
most cost-effective level of treatment is usually to treat
total combined flows. Thus, when a plant is sized, it is not
sized on the basis of dry-weather flow, but rather on the
level of flows from the combined sewer system. As a result,
any reduction in the base dry-weather flow would not significantly affect the sizing of a wastewater treatment plant.

Finally, in speaking of conservation, it must be noted
that conservation, at best, is a stopgap measure. If conservation in a given area is successful, it certainly allows more
time for a community to build up the facilities that would
tender additional water supply. Such practice does not, however, eliminate the need to expand facilities: that is,
growth will take place even though conservation will reduce
the percapita consumption of water. But in any growth area,
the demand for additional water will be present as long as
growth is occurring. Thus, any conservation program is only
one-time effective, and further demand will increase in direct
proportion to the growth of the area.

This fact does not minimize the need for conservation.
Nevertheless, conservation is nothing more than an increase
in use-efficiency of water; and such an increase is expensive.
The goal is to use water more efficiently, and in order to
accomplish this objective we must buy additional equipment,
install additional systems and/or change existing fixtures.
While such practices are, indeed, costly, the end result will
be less water consumption. However, the cost of this water
will not be <u>proportionately</u> reduced. In all likelihood, the
cost will remain fixed and, in many instances, may be increased.

I feel conservation should be presented to the public in
the following manner: Conservation is desirable, it will cost
us money, but it is necessary. It is necessary, because we
are not in a position to waste any resource, especially water.

In incorporating conservation into our national policy on
water resource management, we must direct conservation practices to the areas where conservation is most beneficial, and
we must always remember that the process is a one-time saving.
While it is a method that will provide for the most efficient
use of water, we must pay for it.

Overall, however, the basic philosophy behind the development of any national policy of water resource management
should be one of providing water that is needed, and not one

of eliminating the need. Probably the most serious deficiency
that could be noted in the President's policy is that conservation in some instances is viewed as a means of eliminating
the need for additional water. Many extremes in terms of
water availability are present within this country. We have
certain arid regions where water is not only scarce, it is
unavailable. On the other hand, we have other regions (e.g.,
the Great Lakes region) that account for 30 percent of the
world's total supply of fresh water. So, in developing a
national policy, we should study a long-range, truly national
plan aimed at reusing and redistributing all existing resources.

To achieve this end in some area, new technology will
be needed and must be developed. The absence of any reference
regarding research seems to be a shortcoming in the President's
message. We certainly cannot overlook the need for innovations in technology which research can supply, for if we adopt
the premise that needs must be satisfied rather than eliminated we must admit that existing technology is insufficient
to meet those needs.

As indicated by the welter of discussion on innovative
technology and technology transfer, in public hearings, congressional forums, subcommittee documents, and professional
trade journal articles, a central theme of water conservation
and natural resources policy for the 1980s and beyond is concerned with technology assessment and more intensified research and development. Among the issues which must be addressed are determining risk/benefit tradeoffs in environmental policy; finding effective means of disseminating technological and ecological policy decisions to the public; and involving the academic, industrial, and governmental sectors in
joint water conservation research projects.

There are other challenges facing the technological research community: How can regulated technology be integrated
into management systems? How can it gain overall public ac-
ceptability? These represent other facets of styling innovative technology to meet the criteria of both organizational
practicality and social acceptance of change. How can appropriate accommodation mechanisms be devised to provide a technological base that is conducive both to continued productiv-
ity and environmental preservation? This is yet another important challenge facing the technological research community.
Clearly, innovation in technology is essential to the prosperity of the country. It is also an essential part of the
structuring and initiation of a national policy on nonrenew-
able resources.

Any long-range national water resource policy must also include the requirement for evaluation of all geographic areas in terms of water supply. Once the evaluation is done and critical areas identified in terms of the severity of the need, the next step is to take immediate action to alleviate existing problems. Planning should then be initiated in other areas to avert future crises. Under the immediate actions to be taken in crisis areas, we should consider conservation in its proper context.

Specifically, conservation should be implemented in two areas: First, devices and systems should be installed to physically provide more efficient use of water; for example, reduced flow showers, toilets, and faucets. Also requisite is installation of various systems by industry. These include not only recirculation, but also use of untreated water wherever possible. Second, various incentives for more efficient water use should be promoted. These could include a new type of metering whereby not only customers are metered, but meters are also installed at strategic points in the supply system to determine losses within the system. Alternatively, setting up a sliding-scale rate system--similar to lifeline utility rates (i.e., where the use is higher, the per-unit price is also higher) could also be effective. For larger users of water, a demand rate may be charged to promote more efficient use, and programs could be set up to promote off-peak use of water, especially in deference to the peak load of the local electric system. Simultaneously, part of the immediate action plan should entail steps to increase the water supply. Particular attention should be paid to the feasibility of project implementation so that the greatest benefit to the most people results.

Although other factors are important, they play a secondary role and only are of consequence if other criteria are met. The specific steps vary with the area in question, but certain sources should not be overlooked. A total water resource policy should include all phases of wastewater treatment, as well as phenomena associated with water. The most plentiful untapped supply of water exists in wastewater treatment plants. Unfortunately, technology to economically recirculate effluent from wastewater treatment plants is as yet unavailable. Here is an area in which research could make a major contribution.

Another area where interest and discussion are keen has to do with the possibilities of climate control. Again, the key may be research to produce a viable technology. The possibilities are limitless, if we were to attain even a limited control over climate.

Successful conservation requires adequate, long-term planning. In this context, the federal government should lead in developing a comprehensive national program aimed at the redistribution of our water resources. The total cost of this program would be staggering; however, if the approach were to initiate the program on a step-by-step, cost-effective basis, it certainly could be feasible. This suggested plan does not imply that the federal government should institute a one-blanket policy--as it has a tendency to do, and as it has done in the past. Rather, the program should provide for study of specific areas, and base resource redistribution on the availability or need of water within each area.

In summary, the key elements of a water resource management policy are that it be adequate in scope, that it have the ability to meet actual conditions, that it be structured to meet rather than eliminate needs, that it provide for comprehensive planning to solve short-range as well as long-range problems, and that there be provisions for research. If we approach the problem of water conservation on this basis and resist the temptation to search for absolutes, I am sure that the United States can develop a policy that will accommodate all its present and future needs.

7. Summary of Positions on President Carter's Water Policy Initiatives

Abstract

Recommendations are made on the four Water Policy Initiatives of President Carter: Improving Federal Water Resource Programs, Water Conservation, Improving Federal-State Cooperation and Environmental Protection. Major positions include endorsement of the present Principles and Standards, with concern about adding implied objectives of water conservation and non-structural alternatives per se'. An independent project review body is endorsed, together with considerable strengthening of the Water Resources Council. Concern is expressed about promising too much through water conservation. Positions are taken on government reorganization, integrating planning for water quality and quantity and on research and data needs.

Foreword

This document represents the efforts of the National Water Policy Committee of the American Society of Civil Engineers (ASCE) in developing positions on the Water Policy Initiatives (WPI) issued by President Carter in June 1978. The WPI were preceded by almost a year of intensive review and consideration within the Administration and with segments of the general public, and were stated as being designed to:

(a) Improve Federal water resource programs
(b) Establish Water Conservation as a new national priority
(c) Enhance Federal-State Cooperation
(d) Protect the environment.

Primarily because the early opportunities to comment presented a rapidly moving and ill-defined target, ASCE did

not take specific action during the prior year of review,
until after the issuance of the WPI. In many cases, however,
there is still time to influence future regulations or
legislation. Having had considerable experience in the
implementation of water policy, the engineering profession
can assist in shaping a national water policy and has an
obligation to do so. This will require our keeping abreast
of the actions of the Administration and the Congress and
providing timely, understandable input into the proper
channels.

To implement his water policy, President Carter issued
13 Directives on July 12, 1978. These involve three strategies: new legislation, new regulations under existing
authority, and administrative changes. Bills are being prepared by the Administration for introduction in the 96th
Congress in 1979. A number of preliminary reports on proposed implementation within the Federal agencies have been
issued, under the leadership of the Secretary of the Interior.
Four workshops on the implementation reports that have been
issued were held by the Administration in March 1979, at
Sacramento, Salt Lake City, Omaha and Boston.

Of the issues expected to be given early consideration
by the Administration and the 96th Congress, many have significant technical overtones. The extent to which the full
thrust of the President's water policy is implemented will
depend, in large measure, on the ability of the Congress and
the Administration to take coordinated action.

To accomplish its program of providing inputs to the
Administration's emerging policies, the National Water Policy
Committee of ASCE appointed a Task Committee in July 1978,
with a two-phase objective: Phase 1, to develop an outline
and details of a program that would result in a document
supporting policy positions that ASCE might espouse and,
Phase 2, to complete that document and develop a plan for
effective presentation of the policy positions espoused in
them to the Carter Administration, the Congress, the States,
local entities and the public.

This document represents the results of that program.
It consists of (1) a summary of positions on various issues,
and (2) a series of detailed papers on specific issues
selected by the Task Committeee. Most of the papers were
presented at the Specialty Conference of ASCE's Water
Resources Planning and Management Division in Houston on
February 26-27, 1979. Also included are several additional
papers that were not presented at Houston, but were developed
by individuals at the request of the Task Committee.

Following the Houston Conference, the summary of positions was prepared and reviewed in detail by the National Water Policy Committee. This summary, including the recommendations therein, therefore, represents the position of ASCE's National Water Policy Committee.

The individual papers, which appeared as Appendix A, were given peer review, each by at least one member of the National Water Policy Committee or of its Task Force. However, the papers have not been reviewed by the entire Committee, and have not been modified by it. Therefore, they should not be considered as being the position of the Committee, even though, in the main, they do support the Committee's views.

In addition to the preparation of this document, representatives of the National Water Policy Committee presented a statement at a hearing on water policy of the Subcommittee on Water Resources of the U.S. Senate Committee on Public Works in Denver on September 16, 1978, and at a panel presentation in an Omaha Workshop on March 21, 1978. These statements were included in Appendix B in this document. A representative also participated in the Sacramento Workshop, without the opportunity to participate as a panel member.

Members of the National Water Policy Committee are:

Frederick J. Clarke, Tippetts-Abbett-McCarthy and Stratton, Washington, D.C.

Robert D. Henderson, Tennessee Valley Authority, Knoxville, Tennessee

Victor A. Koelzer, Colorado State University, Fort Collins, Colorado

Theodore M. Schad, National Research Council, Washington, D.C.

Verne H. Scott, University of Calfiornia-Davis, Davis, Calfiornia

Richard W. Karn, Bissell & Karn, Inc., San Leandro, California

Members of the Task Committee on President's Water Policy Initiatives are:

William C. Ackermann, Illinois State Water Survey, Urbana, Illinois, Phase I Chairman

Victor A. Koelzer, Fort Collins, Colorado, Phase
2 Chairman

Theodore M. Schad, Washington, D.C.

Verne H. Scott, Davis, California

Leonard T. Crook, Leonard T. Crook and Associates,
Ann Arbor, Michigan

William Whipple, Jr., Rutgers University, New
Brunswick, New Jersey

Warren Viessman, Jr., Library of Congress,
Washington, D.C.

Harvey O. Banks, Camp Dresser & McKee, Inc.,
Belmont, California

Augustine J. Fredrich, Corps of Engineers,
Washington, D.C.

Summary of the President's Water Policy Initiatives (WPI)

Early in his term, President Carter directed a review
of national water policy by his staff and by heads of Federal
agencies. Seven Federal Task forces were appointed to
develop various options available for solutions of what they
considered to be the principal issues. Inputs and reactions
from the public were solicited. These activities covered
more than a year, culminating in June 1978 when the President
issued the WPI, with the four principal objectives referred
to in the Foreword [1] :

Objective A: Improvement of Federal water resource
programs, through "the use of new criteria and
uniform procedures for the computation of project
costs and benefits." He also proposed "an
expedited interagency review to assure that projects
are assessed rapidly and consistently," together
with "cost-sharing to give States a more meaningful
role in water projects designs and decisions, yet
to protect small States from undue financial
burdens."

Objective B: Establishment of water conservation as a
new national priority, by "directing all Federal

[1] "Remarks of the President on Water Policy," White House
Press Release, June 6, 1978.

agencies to incorporate water conservation requirements in all applicable programs." He further proposed "legislation to allow States the option of
charging more for municipal and industrial water
supplies from Federal reservoirs to encourage conservation, provided that the additional revenue is
returned to the municipality."

Objective C: Enhancement of Federal-State cooperation,
by "proposing grant programs totalling $50 million
to help States plan for their water needs and to
implement water conservation programs." He also
created "a task force with State, local and Federal
officials to examine water-related problems and to
deepen the partnership that this water policy review
has begun."

Objective D: Protection of the environment, by "requiring agencies to enforce environmental statutes more
effectively, and by requiring agencies to fund
environmental mitigation plans at the same time
projects are being built."

The background of the WPI suggests a drive by the
Executive Branch to gain greater control over Federal spending for water projects. They call for more uniform standards
in the evaluation of Federal water projects and increased
cost-sharing by non-Federal participants.

The WPI also appear to show increased Federal concern
over certain aspects of the Nation's water resources, such
as ground water. A further new orientation of water resource
development also seems apparent because of the Administration's proposals for strengthening of environmental considerations in water resources development, increased attention to
non-structural alternatives to development, and establishment
of conservation as the "cornerstone" of future planning.

It is our opinion that an overall review of water policy
from time to time, as undertaken by the President, is in
order. This is in keeping with the long history of development of water policy, which has constantly been evolving, to
reflect the changing needs and aspirations of the American
public.

It should be recognized, however, that the general
thrust of the WPI will probably make water resource development more difficult. Also, it should be noted that the WPI
are silent on the issue of the massive Federal water pollution control program and its relationship to other aspects of
water resources management and development.

As a part of his implementation steps, the President has directed preparation of bills on technical and planning assistance to States, cost-sharing improvements, and State conservation pricing options, for introduction in the 96th Congress in 1979. Effective April 1, 1979, the Water Resources Council was directed to conduct an impartial technical review of pre-authorization reports or proposals and pre-construction plans for Federal and Federally-assisted water and related land resources projects and programs. Within the Federal agencies, 19 inter-agency Task Committees were formed in mid-1978, under the leadership of the Secretary of the Interior.

Significant technical considerations are involved in the WPI. These include conservation, groundwater management, drinking water standards, water project selection, instream flow evaluation, allocation of water supplies, water quality management, water resources planning, consideration of non-structural alternatives, and non-point source pollution.

Our position and recommendations on the policies proposed for each of the four objectives in the WPI are summarized in the following sections.

Objective A.   Improving Federal Water Resource Programs

Principles and Standards

The President has directed modification of the Principles and Standards (P&S) by adding water conservation to the two basic planning objectives of National Economic Development (NED) and Environmental Quality (EQ) as a specific component of both objectives. He also directed that a primarily non-structural plan be formulated "as one alternative whenever structural water projects or programs are planned."

There is a large investment in the present P&S, which were approved in 1973, after a 5-year history of development, testing and debate. In the ensuing six years, a great amount of research has been accomplished on the P&S. Federal agencies have acquired considerable experience in their use. They should not be changed without good reason.

Engineers have always favored measures to conserve water. However, introducing water conservation as a component need of both the NED and EQ objectives would not be in accord with the present framework of the P&S. "Components of the objectives" are defined as the "desired achievement of goods and services and environmental conditions ..., being sought as contributions to the objectives." Examples given are agricultural products, miles of scenic river, etc. These are ends in themselves.

Since water is a renewable resource, water conservation should not be considered an end in itself. Conservation measures may involve additional costs and are justified only if they serve an economic or environmental purpose. As a means to achieving an end, conservation measures should be included, therefore, under "Evaluation and Resource Capabilities," one of the steps in the planning process specified in the P&S in which alternative measures are formulated and considered.

Originally, four objectives rather than the current two were proposed for the P&S. It was perceived that a specific plan might be required for each objective. Experience has shown that even with elimination of two of the four original objectives, the formal planning process is slow, complex and costly. We do, however, favor the multi-objective approach in a two-objective framework. Particularly, the continued use of the benefit-cost ratio as one of the tools for evaluating the National economic objective is appropriate.

We agree with the philosophy of increased consideration of non-structural alternatives. However, to require a specific plan for non-structural measures in all cases is not realistic. Planning would not be cost-effective if it were to require a non-structural plan in those instances in which non-structural approaches are obviously infeasible. Where non-structural alternatives represent a viable approach, they also should be included under "Evaluation of Resource Capabilities," since they represent that part of the planning process.

Specifically, the following is recommended:

(1)   That the basic framework of the existing Principles and Standards be retained, involving only two multi-objectives of National Economic Development (NED) and Environmental Quality (EQ) for which alternative plans must be developed (but providing for a non-structural alternative plan where appropriate).

(2)   That water conservation and consideration of non-structural alternatives be encouraged. However, conservation should not be a specific alternative component of the NED and EQ objectives. Also, a specific alternative plan should not be required for non-structural alternatives in all situations.

Instead, these should be considered specifically in the "Evaluation of Resource Capabilities," a step in the planning process.

Independent Water Project Review

On January 8, 1979, the President directed that, to "ensure .... independent review of Federal water resource programs and projects ..." beginning April 1, 1979, Federal agencies will submit preauthorization project reports or proposals, and preconstruction plans to the Water Resources Council for technical review at least 90 days before submission to the Office of Management and Budget for consideration for the 1981 budget, and for funding in subsequent years.

The independent review by the Water Resources Council is an important first step to improvement of planning. By itself, it may result in improved project and program proposals, as well as in better prioritization of construction authorizations, but it has some limitations. It is "after the fact" with respect to comprehensive, integrated planning. Also, it may prove to be extremely difficult to provide the desired result because it does not restructure the Council to make it truly "independent" or to give the review function "muscle", which we believe is an important step which should follow.

Despite our concerns regarding implementation, we endorse establishment of an independent project review function as a first step. Our thoughts on strengthening the Council, as a next step, follow.

Strengthening the Water Resources Council

Reorganization should be tailored primarily to facilitate effective water resources planning and management, and not be designed for other theoretical organizational management objectives. This requires, first, a look at how effective water resources planning should be accomplished in the present, multi-objective context (i.e. to meet the dual objectives of economic efficiency and environmental quality). Basically, five steps are required:

(1) Hypothesis of goals and objectives

(2) Evaluation of Resource Capabilities and alternative means of achieving goals and objectives

(3) Evaluation of beneficial and adverse consequences (both economic and environmental) of alternative

means of achieving goals and objectives

(4) Presentation of information on resources, alter-
     natives and consequences to decision-makers
     (including the general public) for decisions,
     including a recommended plan

(5) Iteration of process when it is decided that
     modifications of plans are necessary to achieve
     other than postulated goals because of costs or
     other consequences.

The problems which arise in the water resource area fre-
quently do not result from the way in which the Federal Government is organized. They often result from different goals
and aspirations among the American people. These can only be
resolved by good planning.

Ideally, reorganization should follow, not precede, the
establishment of National, regional and State goals and objectives for water and related resources management. Organizational restructuring whould be minimized, directed toward
achieving the goals and objectives, and seek to correct recognized deficiencies in the planning process. Although, in
practice, this may be difficult, it should be followed inso-
far as possible.

There is an urgent need for establishment, at the
Federal level, of an organizational structure with adequate
authority, status, continuity, responsibility and funding to
formulate and recommend policy, and to provide leadership in
achieving comprehensive and integrated planning, protection,
development, and management of water and related resources.
Coordination and joint responsibility among the Federal programs and agencies, and among the Federal activities and
those at the State, regional and local levels must be
improved.

Specifically, we recommend the following:

(1) The Water Resources Council should be reauthorized
     as a Water Resources Commission, with broadened
     powers and responsibilities, as follows:

     (a) It should be an independent agency, with
          commissioners appointed by the President and
          confirmed by the Senate, representing a
          spectrum of views, including representation
          from the public, States and local entities.

(b) The present Council of Representatives of the
Water Resources Council should be retained as
an Advisory Committee. A second Advisory
Committee should be formulated, representing
non-Federal interests.

(c) The staff of the Water Resources Commission
should be sufficient to develop Principles and
Standards, review basin and project plans for
consistency in use of the P&S, develop coordinated planning budgets that are in accord with
basin plans and the P&S, recommend projects
for construction, and make post audits of
projects to assure they conform to intended
purpose and scope (not including technical
design or technical supervision of
construction).

(2) To enhance coordination of water quality and
quantity planning under sections 208 and 209 of
PL 92-500, the entities in Sections 208 and 209
specified as having the responsibility for planning
should have experience in overall water and related
resources planning. At the Federal level, as a
minimum, coordination should be by the Water
Resources Commission. At the field level, the
lead entity should be a River Basin Commission or
a substate entity, as appropriate. (S833 and H2610,
discussed later, would achieve much of this
coordination if the bills are passed.)

Further organizational recommendations are made under
"Federal-State Cooperation" and "Needs for Data and Research."

Cost-Sharing

Civil Engineers are employed by a myriad of Federal,
State, local and other public organizations, as well as by a
variety of private organizations. Each such organization has
its own unique view on cost-sharing policy, largely non-
engineering in nature. We cannot visualize any single view
on specific policies that would be acceptable to all engineers, or to the organizations they represent. Accordingly,
we are restricting our views on this important issue to some
general philosophies which should apply, leaving policies on
specific programs to be developed as appropriate to the
circumstances.

We are in general agreement with the concepts in the
WPI that call for States to increase their participation in

financing of Federal or Federally-assisted water projects, in
instances where determined to be appropriate. However, we
invite attention to the fact that most policies for cost-
sharing have been established for specific functions to
achieve certain National goals or objectives. It follows,
therefore, that changes in cost-sharing formulas should be
made only after examination of the original goals and objectives for adoption of present cost-sharing formulas. We
do not find such examination as a preface to the President's
proposals.

For example, the original objective of the Reclamation
law, under which current subsidies to Federal irrigation
are governed, was to "open the West" and give more connection
between Eastern and Western U.S. This objective has not
been substantially modified throughout the years. While we
are taking no position with regard to current irrigation
subsidies, we can visualize that the route to an Administration position might be made more clear if it first reached a
conclusion as to whether the original goal is still valid,
or should be modified. A similar approach should be used on
cost-sharing policies for other functions.

We are in full agreement with the additional concepts in
the President's proposal that call (1) for reconciliation of
conflicting rules governing various forms of cost-sharing on
similar programs, especially those of flood damage reduction
and (2) consistent with original or currently modified social
goals, for shifts of project cost burdens to identifiable
beneficiaries, where appropriate. We believe, however, that
these basic objectives cannot be achieved by the methods
proposed by the President. To accomplish those objectives,
a more comprehensive and thorough approach must be taken
which will address directly the issues, the inconsistencies
and inequities which have evolved over the years.

The proposal for joint "front-end" financing of projects
with State governments in the amount of 10 percent for
vendible project products and services and 5 percent for non-
vendible services, with retention of existing sharing of
allocated costs, as contemplated in the draft legislation
that has been circulated, is overly complex and should be
avoided. Also, this approach may invite the use of "front-
end" financing as a vehicle to avoid construction; and we
would view such use as improper.

The simplest alternative, where increased State financing is considered appropriate, would be to continue the
practice of full Federal funding of projects by direct
Federal financing (or through an equivalent loan program
when States wish to assume lead roles in planning and

development). This basic policy is set forth in the Water Supply Act of 1958 [P.O. 85-500, Title III; 43 USC 390 (B-D)] for Local-Federal contracts. This approach could require legislation to extend this concept to full or partial recovery, as appropriate, of project outputs at agreed-upon interest rates. States should provide assurances for direct repayment by them, as well as being guarantors, where appropriate, for local governments respecting such outputs as water supply on which user charges are expected. In this manner, States could be more actively involved with the Federal Government (and with local governments) in the planning, development and management of water resources, for which States have considerable constitutional responsibility.

An alternate method, involving a different approach, could be achieved by sharing costs and revenues in proportion to financial investment within an acceptable range, say 10 to 50 percent non-Federal financing, on the basis of project outputs. In view of the National and State-local interests in sound water resources development, the Federal Government should be willing to jointly plan, finance, manage, cost and revenue-share the development of water projects and programs with due consideration for constitutional and established divisions of responsibilities. States and/or local interests would have incentives to support efficient projects on the basis of their financial risks and the opportunity to share in the revenues from vendible outputs. Extensive legislation would be required to develop this policy at both Federal and State levels.

The following recommendations are made:

(1) That cost-sharing guidelines shoud be established that are reasonably consistent among Federal water programs which provide similar services, provided they also are consistent with the social goals to be achieved.

(2) That cost-sharing guidelines should not be the vehicle which strongly influences the alternative plan that is chosen.

(3) That consideration be given to capitalization of operations and maintenance costs for inclusion in the initial cost-sharing divisions on an expected project.

(4) That "front-end" financing not be used as a vehicle to avoid or delay construction, where such

construction is otherwise deemed to be an appropriate instrument in implementing water policy.

Objective B. Water Conservation

The President has stated that conservation should be
the cornerstone of our National water policy, especially
reductions in water demand and elimination of wasteful
practices. The preliminary reports of several Federal task
forces on Water Conservation outlined vigorous programs in
aid of water conservation, but have not taken costs into
account and thus have not provided a sufficient rationale
or proposed decision criteria. It has previously been
observed herein, that it is our view that water conservation
should not be an end in itself, being justified only when
economic efficiency and environmental objectives are
achieved.

The Definition of Water Conservation

The definition of water conservation in the WPI and
Task Force reports is uncertain. An unofficial source has
advised us that the following definition was used in
development of the WPI:

> "Water conservation is defined as wise and efficient
> use of the resource and includes techniques and
> measures to reduce losses and waste, improve
> efficiency in use, and manage runoff and flows; and
> techniques and measures to modify demand."

It appears, from the above definition, that the Administration does not view storage and reregulation as an
acceptable component of conservation. It has been pointed
out, however, that water use and control through storage is
an acceptable component in the Administration's total proposals, through use of the Principles and Standards to evaluate projects. Such projects are a traditional component of
total development that engineers espouse and are endorsed
by this ASCE Committee. With provision by the Administration
for such projects (although admittedly more difficult), it
becomes somewhat academic as to whether the definition of
conservation includes provision of storage, as engineers
have traditionally viewed it.

Further, however, the definition of water conservation
should be viewed in a hydrologic system context. For
example, water conservation at the point of use, such as
reduction in water used in a plumbing fixture or in water
applied for irrigation, has a significant local impact. That

impact may represent a saving in diversion of 100% of the
water conserved. This saving in diversion may be highly
important in the savings in storage and diversion facilities,
municipal water treatment facilities, or in waste treatment
facilities, the cost of which often bear a close correlation
to the amount of water diverted. Thus, significant economic,
as well as some environmental, savings may result.

This is not, however, the whole story. When considered
on a total hydrologic system basis, so-called "savings" by
conservation measures are often an illusion. Water "saved"
through more efficient plumbing is not a saving in the total
stream system, since virtually all of the water used in
plumbing systems is returned, through the sewer system and
the waste treatment plant, to the stream systems. In
Eastern cities, such return flow is often close to 100% of
the water diverted, while in Western cities, it may fall as
low as 70%, due to consumptive use of water through lawn
irrigation.

Similarly, in many systems, much of the water "lost"
in application of irrigation water returns to ground water
and, eventually, to the stream system. Such return flow
is often on the order of 30% of the water diverted.

Where such return flows discharge into fresh water, they
often are reused. Such water conserved at the point of use
does not represent a true system savings. Where return flows
are conserved that would otherwise flow into saline waters,
where they cannot be reused, a true system saving results.

Do the WPI Promise Too Much?

From the above discussion, it can be concluded that to
the extent that return flows are reusable, conservation at
the point of use does not represent a true saving. We fear
that it often is viewed as such, creating an illusion of
savings that are greater than can be realized. There is
danger in promising too much.

While engineers have always concurred in the need for
reduction in demand and in efficient and effective use of
water, we believe that consideration of conservation is too
complex to assume that it is, by definition, always justified.
As indicated earlier, we believe that the Principles and
Standards approach, with the qualifications that have been
stated, is a good one with which to analyze the justification
for conservation measures.

Water Conservation Opportunities

The greatest need and the greatest opportunities for water conservation lie in irrigation in the Western States. Information obtained by the Bureau of Reclamation and Bureau of Indian Affairs indicates that many water conservation opportunities exist on irrigation projects. However, when examined in detail, in accordance with criteria of economic efficiency and environmental quality, about two-thirds of them would cost more than the estimated economic benefits, besides having adverse environmental and energy disadvantages or difficult institutional problems in some cases. In the East, similarly mixed evaluations characterize potential water savings through leakage reduction, re-use of water, inter-connections, and improved private and industrial utilization of water.

A large class of potential improvements, if justified, presumably will be accomplished by the managers of irrigation and municipal water supply systems, provided adequate information is made available. There appears to be little basis for government subsidy of this kind of program, or of mandating execution beyond the limits found feasible by local managers. However, a larger degree of governmental interest appears justified in conservation related to ground water development, institutional and pricing constraints, and drought contingency planning. The question is, which governmental interest is involved?

Ground water development, unlike surface water supply, is largely unregulated. Ground water mining is frequent, and may be justified in some instances. However, decisions on the degree of mining to be allowed should be made only after full investigations of the impacts. In some cases, discontinuance or reduction would have severe economic and social dislocations. The interest of each of the various purveyors exploiting an aquifer may be quite different from that of the public.

Research and planning aspects should be given priority; but where mining is excessive, greater State control will be required. The Federal interest appears restricted to research and data collection because of the traditional role of States of administering water rights. The States must make the ultimate decisions on the degree of mining to be allowed, but must not expect the Federal government to rescue local economies when bad State decisions are made. This implies some Federal interest in planning, at least to the extent of cooperative effort.

In the interest of water conservation, institutional and pricing situations may impose major constraints. The persistence of low water prices, based upon historically low investment costs but far below costs of new supplies, undermines the incentive for water conservation measures. This is particularly true in Western irrigation, but also applies to publicly owned water supply elsewhere. Also, incentive is lacking in the provisions in many State laws in that water rights which are not fully used may be reduced or lost.

Many issues are a matter of local policy. If a Western city wishes to subsidize its municipal water users in order to ensure a "green lawn" image, it should not be required by the Federal government to do otherwise--unless, of course, it is using Federal funds to do so or interstate waters are affected. Thus, pricing and legal constraints are exceedingly important. The modification of legal and institutional barriers will be exceedingly complex and difficult, but some changes, carefully made, seem almost essential to achieve conservation progress.

Drought contingency planning is a field where State and Federal action will be required to protect the public interest. Some purveyors rely upon "normal" stream flows, and market water beyond the yield available during drought, counting upon conservation measures or emergency Federal and State action to come to their rescue at that time. California, for example, weathered its 1977 drought without massive economic losses because the system had reserve capacity. In the future, this approach might not work, if normal operating procedures produce little or no excess reserve in water supply systems, leaving no margin of safety.

Improvised emergency action might include the forced curtailment of mandated "minimum" stream flows. Advance preparations for drought, therefore, should include considerations of emergency need for both water conservation measures and for environmental sacrifices. Among other provisions which should be made in advance of drought emergencies are arrangements for interconnections and exchanges, plus a system of water allocations designed to allow use of stream flows on an interreuptible basis during droughts of specified severity.

Specifically, it is recommended that:

(1) Measures to reduce demand be mandatory to the extent that they are in accord with normal criteria of economic efficiency and environmental quality.

(2) To avoid promising too much, the definition of
     water conservation should consider the effect of
     return flows that may be reusable throughout the
     appropriate surface and ground water systems.

(3) Where costs and benefits are internalized within
     a given system, the final decision as to the
     extent of water conservation practices should be
     left to local management.

(4) For projects involving Federal funds, subsidized
     water prices which fail to provide a proper
     incentive for conservation should be eliminated,
     where possible.

(5) As regards ground water, the Federal emphasis
     should be on research and planning aspects, but
     a substantial degree of State management and
     control will be required to serve the public
     interest. (S833 and H2610, discussed later,
     would help in this recommendation, if passed.)

(6) Local, State and Federal action are required to
     assure proper contingency planning for droughts
     and other emergencies, including provisions for
     water allocation, redistribution, and system
     inter-connections.

Objective C. Federal-State Cooperation

Organizations for Cooperation

Our comments on the need for strengthening Federal
organizations are discussed earlier under Objective A.

The initial statement in the WPI is that "States must
be a focal point for water resource management. The water
reforms are based on this guiding principle." We believe
this statement could be interpreted as being too all-inclusive, if taken literally, and if the Administration includes
planning and funding in "management". While we agree with
the philosophy of a greater shift of responsibilities to the
States, we visualize that major Federal expenditures are, and
will continue to be, needed for water projects. Some
projects are, by nature, interstate or involve Federal
interests; hence, the Federal government must be involved.
Other projects are purely local, or substate, and do not
require even minor State involvement. Regional organizations, involving Federal, State and local membership, are
required for projects involving Federal funding or for other
projects that impact on Federal plans.

Regional organizations should develop basin and regional plans with Federal, State, and local participation. These plans should form the basis for further actions. Regional organizations should help in establishing National policies which are based on regional needs. This would provide the flexibility in National water policy which past studies have demonstrated are almost universally endorsed.

The type of regional organization should not be rigidly set in Washington but should reflect the regional infrastructure, needs, and desires. Where substate organizational structures are needed, they should be developed with a minimum of Federal direction but must be encouraged to cooperate with State and Federal entities in developing their plans. A Federal presence in efforts to develop river basin or regional plans would tend to assure early consideration of National objectives.

The States should strengthen internal organizations, provide top level attention to water and related resources, and cooperate more fully in the development of integrated State goals, objectives, priorities and plans which have Federal, interstate, regional, and sub-state inputs. This is essential to achieve the objectives desired by the States.

The President's directive on January 8, 1979 for an independent review of water resources programs within the Water Resources Council had, as one justification, "to ensure coordinated planning". We question whether the President's proposals will aid in achieving better Federal interagency coordination or in improving Federal-State coordination and cooperation in the water and related resources fields. These must result from integrated planning as proposals for projects are being developed.

To assist the States in strengthening their planning efforts, the WPI proposed two grant programs to the Water Resources Council, each on a 50-50% matching basis. The first was to provide $25 million in matching grants to the States for increased water management programs as originally provided for in Section 301 of the Water Resources Planning Act of 1965. The second was to provide $25 million in matching grants to the States to assist them in providing technical assistance in water conservation measures.

These proposals have now been introduced in the Congress, as S833 and H2610. The funds are proposed to be appropriated to the Water Resources Council, which shall develop guidelines to carry out the proposals. We endorse the $25 million appropriation for water management programs;

particularly, the authority given to the Council in Section 303(a) to approve any program in a State:

> "to address identified goals and objectives of the State water policy, to include the integration of planning and management of water quantity and water quality, as well as the integration of planning and management of ground and surface waters, the protection and management of instream values, taking into account prospective demands for all purposes served through or affected by such activities."

All of the above issues have been identified in this summary as being greatly needed to implement effective water resources planning.

The two bills are less specific on how the funds are to be used for providing technical assistance to implement water conservation measures. While we are in favor of the general concept, we would wish to see the detailed proposals and guidelines before giving full endorsement to this aspect.

In summary we recommend:

(1)   Establishment of regional planning organizations covering all of the Nation's river basins, which would have Federal, State and local participation. The nature of these organizations should be flexible, to allow consideration of representatives that are unique to different areas.

(2)   Implementation measures should be clearly identified in all project plans and be consistent with river basin and sub-state plans.

(3)   State involvement should be enhanced by strengthening internal State organizations and by implementing the authorization for water management programs.

Federal Reserved and Indian Water Rights

Consistent with Federal policies and programs and court decisions, the Federal reserved water rights and Indian water rights should be quantified so that proper planning can proceed, and encouragement given to needed private and public investments in water resources development. This should be completed in a timely manner.

Objective D. Environmental Protection

Soil Conservation

The WPI included directives to encourage more effective
soil conservation through watershed programs of the Soil
Conservation Service (SCS).

The Nation has come to realize during the past 5-10
years that the products of erosion constitute one of the
most serious remaining pollution sources in our streams,
lakes, and estuaries. In many States, it is the most
serious. The sediment resulting from erosion is more than
soil particles, but includes also the nutrients, heavy metals
and pesticides which are attached to the particles.

Conservation practices are not generally economical to
the farmer in the short term. Many farmers maintain that
they cannot afford to adopt them. Appropriations to the
SCS to promote and install better conservation practices are
level or declining. The non-point pollution which results
from erosion is now recognized, but no effective program is
in place to seriously address the problem.

It is recommended that:

(1) The Congress authorize a thorough review of the
     erosion and resulting pollution situation in
     this country.

(2) A program of sufficient scope be developed
     that would have adequate incentives to reduce
     soil losses and pollution to levels which can
     be accepted indefinitely.

Instream Flows

The WPI seeks to protect instream flows for recreation,
water quality, aesthetics and fish and wildlife habitats.
This initiative appears to presume the existemce of a public
right for instream flows. This can pose conflicts with
private rights in both common law and appropriation States.
It should be noted that navigation, hydropower and some
industrial uses may also require instream water flows. Such
uses can usually be evaluated on a purely economic basis.
The concern in this section is limited to environmental and
social values which cannot be so evaluated.

Problems relating to the President's initiatives can be
divided into four major categories. They are: inadequate

and/or conflicting policies at both State and Federal levels, inadequate technology, imperfect cost-sharing mechanisms and fundamental constitutional concerns relating to deprivation of property, or depreciation of property values.

There are a variety of legal and physical actions which can be taken to alleviate existing instream use problems and to provide for future instream needs. The proper mix is site-specific and must be evaluated on a site-by-site basis. Site-specific appraisal requires that instream needs be weighed against other water demands, the relative legal status of competing uses and the physical characteristics of the stream. This requires a comprehensive planning effort not limited solely to project considerations, but one which also focuses on changes needed in policy and legislation, and an administrative contribution to a proposed management scheme.

The scientific base and procedures required to respond to the instream flow issue is not well established. For example, what is the tolerance that different aquatic species have to intermittent or prolonged exposure to heated water discharges from power plants? Or, what social values do we ascribe to preservation of a unique species in a given reach of a stream? The planning effort needs to be supplemented by a research component to establish criteria for determining such environmental and social values of instream flows and the environmental consequences of short-term interruptions in such flows.

The planning effort also must be conscious of cost-sharing mechanisms and to possible changes in such mechanisms. Benefits from instream uses often accrue largely to local residents, or for vacationers visiting a particular area. The incidence of benefits should be reflected in consideration of policies regarding instream benefits. The needs of all publics for water flows, not only the "instream public", need to be considered in benefit considerations and in the planning effort.

The consideration of instream benefits must be responsive to property rights, particulary the rights of appropriators with prior established rights. This considera-tion, and especially the issues of property law related thereto, suggest primary responsibility for the planning exercise necessary for consideration of instream flows, should rest with State governments, who have traditionally been responsible for administering water rights.

The effectiveness of State efforts will be dependent on the availability of adequate Federal grant funds, the nature and extent of the constraints imposed on these grants, and the efforts made to eliminate conflicting policies established by single purpose programs. Federal or State programs which would propose to implement instream flow requirements to the disadvantage of existing property rights, without due compensation, will have little possiblity of success.

We recommend the following:

(1) The growing demand for fulfillment of instream water flows deserves recognition in a balanced water management program, based on a total planning effort weighing resources against needs for instream flows and the needs for other water uses. (S833 and H2610, if passed, would assist in implementing this recommendation.)

(2) The incidence of benefits should be a factor in determining cost-sharing policies.

(3) Since States have primacy in administering water uses, they should have primary responsibility in the required planning effort.

(4) An expanded research component is needed to support the required planning effort, to establish criteria and procedures for estimating environmental and social consequences of maintaining, interrupting or eliminating instream flows for such purposes.

Policy Issues Not Addressed in the WPI

The President's WPI do not include some policy issues that we consider to be of major importance. These include water quality planning, integration of surface and ground water management, and research and data needs. Our position on these issues follow.

Water Quality Planning

Pollution control grants, which presently dominate Federal water expenditures, are exempted from use of the procedures of the P&S. This is inconsistent. As far as practicable, they should be placed in the same analytical framework as other water projects with respect to impacts, non-structural alternatives and cost-effectiveness. The lack of coordination between water quality and water quantity issues was emphasized as a serious problem in the President's message to Congress of May 23, 1977, but was not referred to in the President's WPI of June, 1978. It is too important to be neglected.

The construction grants program of the EPA is the largest component of Federal water resources expenditures. It is managed virtually without relationship to other Federal planning, without formal economic justification, and with only a rather indirect and loose relationship to cost-effectiveness criteria. The deficiencies in this decision-making approach have been emphasized by engineers, economists, and other analysts for several years past.

There are three possible fields for action to improve this situation: first, the relationship between planning and decision making; second, the criteria for planning; and third, the institutional arrangement for planning.

Regarding the first possible field of action, a clear-cut answer can be proposed. It is considered that for a program which, if fully implemented, would cost hundreds of billions of dollars, formal planning should be undertaken before major decisions are made. This planning should follow a meaningful process and not be purely pro forma. Advanced waste treatment of effluents, and the degree thereof, should be justified by for a formal planning process, such as those of Sections 208 or 209 of PL 92-500, prior to being required.

As regard criteria for planning, the current revision of "Principles and Standards" of the Water Resources Council should provide appropriate criteria for water quality planning. Until an approach that incorporates economic and environmental efficiency can be developed, such planning should be based upon established water quality goals and a cost-effectiveness approach. Although this approach is theoretically postulated under EPA regulations, the problem is that "goals" are arbitrarily established. Multiple-purpose projects involving water quality would require a special criterion to be devised by the Water Resources Commission, which we have proposed, as well as an improved inter-agency planning effort.

As regards planning arrangements, Federal support should be given to establishment of substate planning agencies, in addition to interstate entities, designed to carry out area-wide quality planning such as that of Section 208. In addition, any required areawide planning for stormwater management, stream erosion, and water supply needs to be fully coordinated by such agencies. Again, EPA regulations provide for such coordination, but funds are not being provided. Such planning should be oriented to develop the most advantageous programs for local and State support, as well as Federal support. The agencies would preferably operate under the overview and coordination of the Water Resources Commission which we propose, with appropriate relationship to the various other Federal, State and local agencies as their respective interests might appear in the various parts of the country.

Section 209, which involves integration of water quality and water quantity planning, should be implemented and made to work, in a manner that would be consistent with improving State primacy in such matters. Action should be taken to require EPA to prepare or help to prepare formal river basin water quality plans, as a portion of river basin plans. If a decision is to be taken, for example, to make the Potomac estuary fully fishable and swimmable, the plans for doing so, the costs to all concerned, and the consequences (beneficial and adverse) should be spelled out in river basin plans.

Finally, action should be taken to strengthen comprehensive planning with coordination by the proposed Water Resources Commission, under Section 209 of PL 92-500, which specifically refers to the provisions of PL 89-80. Water quality plans of EPA should be required to be consistent with such comprehensive planning.

The concept of elimination of discharge of pollutants in PL 92-500 was established as a goal, not necessarily as a standard that must be achieved in all cases. It is now generally accepted that, although the goal still remains, the achievement of that goal is, in most instances, not physically possible nor desirable from an economic viewpoint. Effectiveness in approaching such goals can be most appropriately gauged by the frequency of compliance with the standards. This is especially true in projects with large variability in pollutant loading, such as those involving storm runoff. Costs and frequency of compliance can be compared so that an optimum cost performance (cost-effective) project is selected. Non-structural and non-conventional approaches which are based on frequency would probably see more acceptance of water quality standards and regulations.

The WPI do not appear to include provisions for non-structural alternatives in water quality planning, such as the use of the natural assimilative capacity of streams, to be used in lieu of unnecessary or more costly degrees of treatment. Much of the inconsistency and inequity between

structural and non-structural planning approaches can be
remedied by formalizing planning coordination between EPA and
the Water Resources Commission, so these two agencies can
work toward consistency in planning guidelines for Federal
water programs. Similar approaches can be used to mitigate
inconsistencies in other programs, such as flood control.
The WPI do not address these issues.

The following specific recommendations are made:

(1)   That all grants for pollution control be analyzed
      according to the basic objectives of economic
      efficiency and environmental quality outlined
      in the P&S. Appropriate revisions in legisla-
      tion and in the P&S would be necessary.

(2)   That advanced waste treatment grants, before
      being funded by EPA, be justified by a formal
      planning process, such as those in Sections
      208 or 209 of PL 92-500. Strengthening of
      comprehensive planning under the proposed Water
      Resources Commission will be necessary, together
      with obtaining consistency between river basin
      and EPA planning.

(3)   Realistic water quality standards and regulations
      should be established which are based upon
      frequency which allows for variability caused
      by weather induced loading. (The WPI does not
      address this issue.)

Integration of Surface and Ground Water Management

It is well known that surface water and ground water
cannot always be viewed in isolation, since at various times
in the hydrologic cycle, there is physical interchange between the two. There is justification for this separation,
in many cases, of supplies for small communities (for example,
in many areas of Illinois) where the municipal supply is
rather distinctly from either ground or surface water and
there is little interchange between the two that is of practical significance, from a supply viewpoint. Yet, they are
often treated as separate entities in many instances of
larger supplies, such as for irrigation, where such separate
consideration is inappropriate. In these cases, the separate
consideration relates to the laws pertaining to their use, to
the institutions which deal with them and, sometimes, to scientific or engineering procedures which are inadequate for
planning their use.

Many of the problems of ground water use result from an inadequate understanding of the physical principles of aquifer systems. Generally speaking, there are less data available for ground water systems than for surface water. The ability to model ground water systems is not as well developed for surface water, and data cannot be transferred between areas of hydrologic similarity as easily (if at all) as they can for surface water. This, in turn, results in an inadequate understanding of the economics and principles of interaction between ground and surface water systems.

Only a few States have water rights laws which recognize the interaction of surface and ground water. Many have laws governing surface water rights, but in most, the laws pertaining to use of ground water are either indefinite or overly permissive in pumping. A few States have encountered difficulty in protecting surface water rights because of excessive ground water pumping and have had to move toward conjunctive use laws. Improved laws are needed in many areas, and since water rights are a matter of State primacy, more States should move in that direction, where needed.

Efficient integration of surface and ground water would, ideally, permit drawdown of the aquifer during low flow periods and the use of the aquifer for storage of excess surface flows at times of high surface runoff. Difficulties in understanding or in obtaining data on response time or capacity of aquifers may prevent efficient use of an aquifer as a storage vehicle for such surplus surface water. In some instances, the transmissability limits movement in an aquifer and inhibits its use for storage. In other cases, State laws are restrictive, preventing pumping of the aquifer in a manner to create storage. The situation is too complex and site-specific to allow generalization but it may be possible to allow use of some aquifers as a storage vehicle to achieve better integration of surface and ground water use. However, it should be approached cautiously, on a case-by-case basis, to avoid injudicious mining.

To achieve economic efficiency, water should be allocated so the net marginal value among users over time is more equitable. This is rarely the case with relation to surface and ground water use, because of differences in water rights law and differences in method of development and financing. Greater consideration of conjunctive use of surface and ground water would yield significant benefits in many instances of large uses.

A third problem is the degradation of ground water, which may not be restricted to the large user, but may occur in supplies for small communities as well. Since degradation is not visible, and often remains undetected until there is a crisis, it is often neglected. However, continuing a "hands off" policy on ground water quality will only encourage continued procrastination. To limit interest to regulating point pollution sources leaves much of the problem unsolved. On the other hand, the arbitrary "standards" approach of the Federal Water Pollution Control act, with no regard to cost, should be avoided. Good research is greatly needed to allow alternate approaches.

The problems that have been discussed will not be easy to solve. However, effective planning and management of conjunctive use of aquifers and surface water sources will contribute to their solution, in many instances. Many water authorities feel they have taken steps toward conjunctive use programs, such as artificial recharge and combined ground water-surface water systems; however, very few of these programs are obtaining maximum benefits from the combined systems. In most places, the limiting factor is inadequate ground water policy, management, and control.

Four policy positions are recommended:

(1) The Federal Government should encourage States to update and modernize their water institutions and laws to facilitate more efficient planning and management of ground water and surface water systems.

(2) The Federal Government should encourage State programs to protect ground water quality, including systematic monitoring.

(3) The ground water data base needs to be strengthened, with greater coordination of activities of Federal, State and local agencies in the data collection and updating program.

(4) Increased research is needed in areas of optimal data collection networks, management and institutional frameworks, legal systems, economic incentives, and optimal water systems management.

Research and Data Needs

Changes in water resources policy, such as indicated in the WPI, must necessarily require new research directions and a strong data program to find improved means of achieving the desired goals. These have been alluded to in a number of the issues previously discussed. These research and data needs are not enunciated in the WPI.

The current reordering of our National water resources programs, priorities, responsibilities and procedures cannot stand for all time, but must remain flexible and responsive to natural and social change and to future refinements in these aspects. Such refinements will come in large measure from the findings of a balanced, timely, efficient, and high quality research program. The real questions involving research are the budgets and relative priorities for basic research, as compared with mission-oriented research. In recent years, there has been little interagency prioritization of research, and little interagency coordination. The present administration is attempting to strengthen these aspects, but care must be taken to avoid a degree of control that is stifling to initiative. More attention should be given to research fields which overlap more than one Federal agency program, or which concern problems that are the primary responsibility of States and local agencies rather than the Federal agencies.

Water research received a great deal of attention at the time of establishment of Water Resources Research Institutes in each State in 1962-64. Since that time, there has been deteriorating attention. The research system put in place in 1962-64 has had its mandate eroded and National attention has diminished. The erosion should be stopped and a new impetus established. The results of numerous research-needs reports are available as initial guidance for a new focus on a program of needed research.

Water resources data programs do not appear to have received direct attention in the deliberations or statement of the President's WPI. Studies and reports which have appeared subsequent to June 6, 1978, reflect only modest attention to the data requirements of new policy directions. There is a continuing need for centralized coordination of basic data collection and storage, with uniform standards of collection and procession. Subcommittees of the Water Resources Council have been very effective in coordinating water data in the past. A new focus, under the proposed Water Resources Commission, should place new attention to coordinated data that are collected, including demographic, socio-economic and environmental data which reflect the present multi-objective approach to planning.

We recommend that:

(1)   The Administration affirm the importance of a strong program of water resources research which is scientifically based, coordinated, visible, and responsive to current water problems of the

Nation. It should have strong ties to the
Water Resources Commission recommended
earlier.

(2) A continuous National assessment of water
     research needs be developed. This should
     include prioritization and budgetary require-
     ments for completing needed research in
     time to be of value. Provision should be
     made for input as to research needs from
     State and regional agencies and for more
     research into problems that are primarily of
     State and local concern. A mechanism should
     also be established for this process to
     directly and effectively influence program
     planning processes of the Executive and
     Legislative Branches.

(3) Strong Federal and National coordinated
     programs of water resources data acquisition
     and availability are urged, including related
     demographic, socio-economic and environmental
     data which reflect the current multi-objective
     approach to water resources planning.

(4) New data agencies should not be established;
     instead, existing agencies should be
     strengthened, with coordination by the proposed
     Water Resources Commission.

Federal Water Policy Initiatives

FEDERAL WATER POLICY INITIATIVES

MESSAGE

FROM

THE PRESIDENT OF THE UNITED STATES

TRANSMITTING

INITIATIVES TO IMPROVE THE FEDERAL WATER POLICY, PURSUANT TO SECTION 80 OF THE WATER RESOURCES PLANNING ACT OF 1974

JUNE 6, 1978.—Message referred to the Committee of the Whole House on the State of the Union and ordered to be printed

---

U.S. GOVERNMENT PRINTING OFFICE

29–011   WASHINGTON : 1978

To the Congress of the United States:

I am today sending to Congress water policy initiatives designed to:
—Improve planning and efficient management of Federal water resource programs to prevent waste and to permit necessary water
projects which are cost-effective, safe and environmentally sound
to move forward expeditiously;
—Provide a new, national emphasis on water conservation;
—Enhance Federal-State cooperation and improved State water resources planning; and
—Increase attention to environmental quality.

None of the initiatives would impose any new Federal regulatory
program for water management.

Last year, I directed the Water Resources Council, the Office of Management and Budget and the Council on Environmental Quality, under
the chairmanship of Secretary Cecil Andrus, to make a comprehensive
review of Federal water policy and to recommend proposed reforms.

This new water policy results from their review, the study of water
policy ordered by the Congress in Section 80 of the Water Resources
Planning Act of 1974 and our extensive consultations with members of
Congress, State, county, city and other local officials and the public.

Water is an essential resource, and over the years, the programs of
the Bureau of Reclamation, the Corps of Engineers, the Soil Conservation Service and the Tennessee Valley Authority have helped permit a dramatic improvement in American agriculture, have provided
irrigation water essential to the development of the West, and have developed community flood protection, electric power, navigation and
recreation throughout the Nation.

I ordered this review of water policies and programs because of my
concern that while Federal water resources programs have been of
great benefit to our Nation, they are today plagued with problems and
inefficiencies. In the course of this water policy review we found that:
—Twenty-five separate Federal agencies spend more than $10 bil-
lion per year on water resources projects and related programs.
—These projects often are planned without a uniform, standard
basis for estimating benefits and costs.
—States are primarily responsible for water policy within their
boundaries, yet are not integrally involved in setting priorities
and sharing in Federal project planning and funding.
—There is a $34 billion backlog of authorized or uncompleted
projects.
—Some water projects are unsafe or environmentally unwise and
have caused losses of natural streams and rivers, fish and wildlife
habitat and recreational opportunities.

The study also found that water conservation has not been addressed
at a national level even though we have pressing water supply problems. Of 106 watershed subregions in the country, 21 already have
severe water shortages. By the year 2000 this number could increase to

(1)

39 subregions. The Nation's cities are also beginning to experience water shortage problems which can only be solved at very high cost. In some areas, precious groundwater supplies are also being depleted at a faster rate than they are replenished. In many cases an effective water conservation program could play a key role in alleviating these problems.

These water policy initiatives will make the Federal Government's water programs more efficient and responsive in meeting the Nation's water-related needs. They are designed to build on fundamentally sound statutes and on the Principles and Standards which govern the planning and development of Federal water projects, and also to enhance the role of the States, where the primary responsibilities for water policy must lie. For the first time, the Federal Government will work with State and local governments and exert needed national leadership in the effort to conserve water. Above all, these policy reforms will encourage water projects which are economically and environmentally sound and will avoid projects which are wasteful or which benefit a few at the expense of many.

Across the Nation there is remarkable diversity in the role water plays. Over most of the West, water is scarce and must be managed carefully—and detailed traditions and laws have grown up to govern the use of water. In other parts of the country, flooding is more of a problem than drought, and in many areas, plentiful water resources have offered opportunities for hydroelectric power and navigation. In the urban areas of our Nation, water supply systems are the major concern—particularly where antiquated systems need rehabilitation in order to conserve water and assure continued economic growth.

Everywhere, water is fundamental to environmental quality. Clean drinking water, recreation, wildlife and beautiful natural areas depend on protection of our water resources.

Given this diversity, Federal water policy cannot attempt to prescribe water use patterns for the country. Nor should the Federal Government preempt the primary responsibility of the States for water management and allocation. For those reasons, these water policy reforms will *not* preempt State or local water responsibilities. Yet water policy is an important national concern, and the Federal Government has major responsibilities to exercise leadership, to protect the environment and to develop and maintain hydroelectric power, irrigated agriculture, flood control and navigation.

The primary focus of the proposals is on the water resources programs of the Corps of Engineers, the Bureau of Reclamation, the Soil Conservation Service and the Tennessee Valley Authority, where annual water program budgets total approximately $3.75 billion. These agencies perform the Federal Government's water resource development programs. In addition, a number of Federal agencies with water-related responsibilities will be affected by this water policy.

I am charging Secretary Andrus with the lead responsibility to see that these initiatives are carried out promptly and fully. With the assistance of the Office of Management and Budget and the Council on Environmental Quality, he will be responsible for working with the other Federal agencies, the Congress, State and local governments and the public to assure proper implementation of this policy and to make appropriate recommendations for reform in the future.

SPECIFIC INITIATIVES

IMPROVING FEDERAL WATER RESOURCE PROGRAMS

The Federal Government has played a vital role in developing the water resources of the United States. It is essential that Federal water programs be updated and better coordinated if they are to continue to serve the nation in the best way possible. The reforms I am proposing are designed to modernize and improve the coordination of Federal water programs. In addition, in a few days, I will also be sending to the Congress a Budget amendment proposing funding for a number of new water project construction and planning starts. These projects meet the criteria I am announcing today. This is the first time the Executive Branch has proposed new water project starts since Fiscal Year 1975, four years ago.

The actions I am taking include:

A directive to the Water Resources Council to improve the implementation of the Principles and Standards governing the planning of Federal water projects. The basic planning objectives of the Principles and Standards—national economic development and environmental quality—should be retained and given equal emphasis. In addition, the implementation of the Principles and Standards should be improved by:

—Adding water conservation as a specific component of both the economic and environmental objectives;

—Requiring the explicit formulation and consideration of a primarily non-structural plan as one alternative whenever structural water projects or programs are planned;

—Instituting consistent, specific procedures for calculating benefits and costs in compliance with the Principles and Standards and other applicable planning and evaluation requirements. Benefit-cost analyses have not been uniformly applied by Federal agencies, and in some cases benefits have been improperly recognized, "double-counted" or included when inconsistent with federal policy or sound economic rationale. I am directing the Water Resources Council to prepare within 12 months a manual which ensures that benefits and costs are calculated using the best techniques and provides for consistent application of the Principles and Standards and other requirements;

—Ensuring that water projects have been planned in accordance with the Principles and Standards and other planning requirements by creating, by Executive Order, a project review function located in the Water Resources Council. A professional staff will ensure an impartial review of pre-construction project plans for their consistency with established planning and benefit-cost analysis procedures and applicable requirements. They will report on compliance with these requirements to agency heads, who will include their report, together with the agency recommendations, to the Office of Management and Budget. Project reviews will be completed within 60 days, before the Cabinet officer makes his or her Budget request for the coming fiscal year. Responsibility will rest with the Cabinet officer for Budget requests to the Office of Management and Budget, but timely independent review will be provided. This review must be completed within the same budget

cycle in which the Cabinet Officer intends to make Budget requests
so that the process results in no delay.
—The manual, the Principles and Standards requirements and the
independent review process will apply to all authorized projects
(and separable project features) not yet under construction.
Establishment of the following criteria for setting priorities each
year among the water projects eligible for funding or authorization,
which will form the basis of my decisions on specific water projects.
—Projects should have net national economic benefits unless there
are environmental benefits which clearly more than compensate
for any economic deficit. Net adverse environmental consequences
should be significantly outweighed by economic benefits. Generally, projects with higher benefit/cost ratios and fewer adverse
environmental consequences will be given priority within the
limits of available funds.
—Projects should have widely distributed benefits.
—Projects should stress water conservation and appropriate non-
structural measures.
—Projects should have no significant safety problems involving design, construction or operation.
—There should be evidence of active public support including support by State and local officials.
—Projects will be given expedited consideration where State governments assume a share of costs over and above existing
cost-sharing.
—There should be no significant international or inter-governmental
problems.
—Where vendible outputs are involved preference should be given
to projects which provide for greater recovery of Federal and
State costs, consistent with project purposes.
—The project's problem assessment, environmental impacts, costs
and benefits should be based on up-to-date conditions (planning
should not be obsolete).
—Projects should be in compliance with all relevant environmental
statutes.
—Funding for mitigation of fish and wildlife damages should be
provided concurrently and proportionately with construction
funding.
Preparation of a legislative proposal for improving cost-sharing for
water projects. Improved cost-sharing will allow States to participate
more actively in project decisions and will remove biases in the existing system against non-structural flood control measures. These
changes will help assure project merit. This proposal, based on the
study required by Section 80 of Public Law 93–251, has two parts:
—participation of States in the financing of Federal water project
construction. For project purposes with vendible outputs (such
as water supply or hydroelectric power), States would contribute
10 percent of the costs, proportionate to and phased with Federal
appropriations. Revenues would be returned to the States proportionate to their contribution. For project purposes without
vendible outputs (such as flood control), the State financing share
would be 5 percent. There would be a cap on State participation
per project per year of ¼ of 1 percent of the State's general rev-

enues so that a small State would not be precluded from having a very large project located in it. Where project benefits accrue to more than one State, State contributions would be calculated accordingly, but if a benefiting State did not choose to participate in cost-sharing, its share could be paid by other participating States. This State cost-sharing proposal would apply on a mandatory basis to projects not yet authorized. However, for projects in the authorized backlog, States which voluntarily enter into these cost-sharing arrangements will achieve expedited Executive Branch consideration and priority for project funding, as long as other project planning requirements are met. Soil Conservation Service projects will be completely exempt from this State cost-sharing proposal.

equalizing cost-sharing for structural and non-structural flood control alternatives. There is existing authority for 80 percent–20 percent Federal/non-Federal cost-sharing for non-structural flood control measures (including in-kind contributions such as land and easements). I will begin approving non-structural flood control projects with this funding arrangement and will propose that a parallel cost-sharing requirement (including in-kind contributions) be enacted for structural flood control measures, which currently have a multiplicity of cost-sharing rules.

Another policy issue raised in section 80 of Public Law 93–251 is that of the appropriate discount rate for computing the present value of future estimated economic benefits of water projects. After careful consideration of a range of options I have decided that the currently legislated discount rate formula is reasonable, and I am therefore recommending that no change be made in the current formula. Nor will I recommend retroactive changes in the discount rate for currently authorized projects.

WATER CONSERVATION

Managing our vital water resources depends on a balance of supply, demand and wise use. Using water more efficiently is often cheaper and less damaging to the environment than developing additional supplies. While increases in supply will still be necessary, these reforms places emphasis on water conservation and make clear that this is now a national priority.

In addition to adding the consideration of water conservation to the Principles and Standards, the initiatives I am taking include:

Directives to all Federal agencies with programs which affect water supply or consumption to encourage water conservation, including:
  —Making appropriate community water conservation measures a condition of the water supply and wastewater treatment grant and loan programs of the Environmental Protection Agency, the Department of Agriculture and the Department of Commerce;
  —Integrating water conservation requirements into the housing assistance programs of the Department of Housing and Urban Development, the Veterans Administration and the Department of Agriculture;
  —Providing technical assistance to farmers and urban dwellers on how to conserve water through existing programs of the Department of Agriculture, the Department of Interior and the Department of Housing and Urban Development;

—Requiring development of water conservation programs as a condition of contracts for storage or delivery of municipal and industrial water supplies from federal projects;

—Requiring the General Services Administration, in consultation with affected agencies, to establish water conservation goals and standards in Federal buildings and facilities;

—Encouraging water conservation in the agricultural assistance programs of the Department of Agriculture and the Department of Interior which affect water consumption in water-short areas; and

—Requesting all Federal agencies to examine their programs and policies so that they can implement appropriate measures to increase water conservation and re-use.

A directive to the Secretary of the Interior to improve the implementation of irrigation repayment and water service contract procedures under existing authorities of the Bureau of Reclamation. The Secretary will:

—Require that new and renegotiated contracts include provisions for recalculation and renegotiation of water rates every five years. This will replace the previous practice of 40-year contracts which often do not reflect inflation and thus do not meet the beneficiaries' repayment obligations;

—Under existing authority add provisions to recover operation and maintenance costs when existing contracts are renegotiated, or earlier where existing contracts have adjustment clauses;

—More precisely calculate and implement the "ability to pay" provision in existing law which governs recovery of a portion of project capital costs.

Preparation of legislation to allow States the option of requiring higher prices for municipal and industrial water supplies from Federal projects in order to promote conservation, provided that State revenues in excess of Federal costs would be returned to municipalities or other public water supply entities for use in water conservation or rehabilitation of water supply systems.

FEDERAL-STATE COOPERATION

States must be the focal point for water resource management. The water reforms are based on this guiding principle. Therefore, I am taking several initiatives to strengthen Federal-State relations in the water policy area and to develop a new, creative partnership. In addition to proposing that States increase their roles and responsibilities in water resources development through cost-sharing, the actions I am taking include:

Proposing a substantial increase from $3 million to $25 million annually in the funding of State water planning under the existing 50 percent-50 percent matching program administered by the Water Resources Council. State water planning would integrate water management and implementation programs which emphasize water conservation and which are tailored to each State's needs including assessment of water delivery system rehabilitation needs and development of programs to protect and manage groundwater and instream flows.

Preparation of legislation to provide $25 million annually in
50 percent–50 percent matching grant assistance to States to implement water conservation technical assistance programs. These
funds could be passed through to counties and cities for use in
urban or rural water conservation programs. This program will
be administered by the Water Resources Council in conjunction
with matching grants for water resources planning.

Working with Governors to create a Task Force of Federal,
State, county, city and other local officials to continue to address
water-related problems. The administrative actions and legislative proposals in this Message are designed to initiate sound water
management policy at the national level. However, the Federal
government must work closely with the States, and with local
governments as well, to continue identifying and examining water-
related problems and to help implement the initiatives I am announcing today. This Task Force will be a continuing guide as
we implement the water policy reforms and will ensure that the
State and local role in our Nation's water policy is constant and
meaningful.

An instruction to Federal agencies to work promptly and expeditiously to inventory and quantify Federal reserved and Indian water rights. In several areas of the country, States have
been unable to allocate water because these rights have not been
determined. This quantification effort should focus first on high
priority areas, should involve close consultation with the States
and water users and should emphasize negotiations rather than
litigation wherever possible.

ENVIRONMENTAL PROTECTION

Water is a basic requirement for human survival, is necessary for
economic growth and prosperity, and is fundamental to protecting
the natural environment. Existing environmental statutes relating to
water and water projects generally are adequate, but these laws must
be consistently applied and effectively enforced to achieve their purposes. Sensitivity to environmental protection must be an important
aspect of all water-related planning and management decisions. I
am particularly concerned about the need to improve the protection
of instream flows and to evolve careful management of our nation's
precious groundwater supplies, which are threatened by depletion and
contamination.

My initiatives in this area include the following:

A directive to the Secretary of the Interior and other Federal
agency heads to implement vigorously the Fish and Wildlife Coordination Act, the Historic Preservation Act and other environ-
mantal statutes. Federal agencies will prepare formal implementing procedures for the Fish and Wildlife Coordination Act and
other statutes where appropriate. Affected agencies will prepare
reports on compliance with environmental statutes on a project-
by-project basis for inclusion in annual submissions to the Office
of Management and Budget.

A directive to agency heads requiring them to include desig-
nated funds for environmental mitigation in water project appro-

priation requests to provide for concurrent and proportionate expenditure of mitigation funds.

Accelerated implementation of Executive Order No. 11988 on floodplain management. This Order requires agencies to protect floodplains and to reduce risks of flood losses by not conducting, supporting or allowing actions in floodplains unless there are no practicable alternatives. Agency implementation is behind schedule and must be expedited.

A directive to the Secretaries of Army, Commerce, Housing and Urban Development and Interior to help reduce flood damages through acquisition of flood-prone land and property, where consistent with primary program purposes.

A directive to the Secretary of Agriculture to encourage more effective soil and water conservation through watershed programs of the Soil Conservation Service by:

—Working with the Fish and Wildlife Service to apply fully the recently-adopted stream channel modification guidelines;
—Encouraging accelerated land treatment measures prior to funding of structural measures on watershed projects, and making appropriate land treatment measures eligible for Federal cost-sharing;
—Establishing periodic post-project monitoring to ensure implementation of land treatment and operation and maintenance activities specified in the work plan and to provide information helpful in improving the design of future projects.

A directive to Federal agency heads to provide increased cooperation with States and leadership in maintaining instream flows and protecting groundwater through joint assessment of needs, increased assistance in the gathering and sharing of data, appropriate design and operation of Federal water facilities, and other means. I also call upon the Governors and the Congress to work with Federal agencies to protect the fish and wildlife and other values associated with adequate instream flows. New and existing projects should be planned and operated to protect instream flows, consistent with State law and in close consultation with States. Where prior commitments and economic feasibility permit, amendments to authorizing statutes should be sought in order to provide for streamflow maintenance.

CONCLUSION

These initiatives establish the goals and the framework for water policy reform. They do so without impinging on the rights of States and by calling for a closer partnership among the Federal, State, county, city and other local levels of government. I want to work with the Congress, State and local governments and the public to implement this policy. Together we can protect and manage our nation's water resources, putting water to use for society's benefit, preserving our rivers and streams for future generations of Americans, and averting critical water shortages in the future through adequate supply, conservation and wise planning.

JIMMY CARTER.

The WHITE HOUSE, *June 6, 1978.*

○

Index